Safety and Consent for Kids and Teens with Autism or Special Needs

SAFETY and CONSENT for KIDS and TEENS with AUTISM or SPECIAL NEEDS

— A Parents' Guide —

DEBRA S. JACOBS

Jessica Kingsley *Publishers*
London and Philadelphia

First published in 2019
by Jessica Kingsley Publishers
73 Collier Street
London N1 9BE, UK
and
400 Market Street, Suite 400
Philadelphia, PA 19106, USA

www.jkp.com

Library of Congress Cataloging in Publication Data
A CIP catalog record for this book is available from the Library of Congress

British Library Cataloguing in Publication Data
A CIP catalogue record for this book is available from the British Library

ISBN 978 1 78592 828 4
eISBN 978 1 78450 970 5

Printed and bound in Great Britain

This book is dedicated to all survivors. Do not allow the past to define your future.

DSJ, Tucson, AZ, 2018

Contents

Acknowledgements

I would like to thank, in no particular order, the following people who were instrumental in my research for this work: Linda Clay of the Children's Advocacy Center in Tucson, Timalee Nevels of Girl Scouts of Southern Arizona, Susan Buxbaum, Laura Gutowski, Mary Sledbodnik, Lisa Sternberg, and my dear cheering squad, Elissa Erly, Chris Loya, Arlene Stamp, Brenda Tobin, Scott Tobin, and Jim Jacobs, my husband, whose support is never flagging.

Thank you all in helping me to fulfill my intention of *Tikkun olam* (healing the world) as much as I am able.

Notes on the text

This book uses female pronouns when describing victims of coercion. This has been done for the sake of continuity and by no means intends to exclude male victims of sexual molestation or abuse of any kind. Although the male pronoun is used for the perpetrator of abuse, this by no means excludes the fact that women are also perpetrators of abuse and molestation as well.

In addition to being a valuable resource for parents, this book is appropriate for use by the layperson and professional alike. I encourage the addition of this book into the course work of education professionals, clergy, coaches, and anyone else who will be working with children with any variation of ability.

CHAPTER 1

Introduction

All children must be kept safe from molestation[1] and abuse. Children with special needs are exceptionally vulnerable, with statistics reporting them to be three times as likely to be molested as their typically developing peers; exceptional preventive measures therefore need to be taken to keep them safe.

The United Nations (UN) Convention on the Rights of the Child (1989) states that children with special needs have all the rights of their typically developing peers as "members of the human family." This international document clearly states that it must be a priority of all countries that children are provided with a safe environment and education so that they are able to reach their fullest potential.

The rights of children with special needs are specifically delineated within the UN Convention, and the inference of this demarcation is that children with special needs must have the appropriate education, care, and environment to reach their highest possible levels of function and social engagement.

The current educational emphasis is on inclusion, encouraging children with special needs to develop social relationships with typically developing peers and learning appropriate behavior, and in my experience when working with children, I have seen wonderful relationships flourish as a

---

1   Molestation refers to any sort of harassment or abuse against another person.

result of this inclusive practice. I have also witnessed children with special needs who desperately crave the attention and acceptance of other students behaving in attention-seeking and often outrageous ways to garner that attention – for example, the student with special needs who witnesses her typical peer secretly passing a note, or in older grades, furtively kissing or touching another student in a quiet place in the library. She witnesses these behaviors and may come to the conclusion that this is an appropriate way to act because the typical students are engaged in this activity. She does not have the skill or the sophistication to discern that not everything her typical peers do is acceptable or appropriate nor should be imitated.

At times, the world we live in is a threatening and dangerous place. Children with special needs are particularly vulnerable to adults and other children who do not always have good intentions, all too often becoming victims of abuse and molestation, or they may even be coerced to commit crimes. Children with special needs may participate in behaviors they do not fully understand, convinced to do these acts on the promise of treats, fun times, or help for their families, or simply in the name of friendship. In other instances they may be threatened if they do not comply with a stronger child or adult, with threats against themselves or family members.

As an occupational therapist I have worked with hundreds of children over the years who have suffered from abuse and molestation. I felt it was important to share my expertise to help increase the awareness of this reality and decrease the numbers of children who suffer this fate. These pages provide techniques and ideas that can be incorporated into daily life and allow children to be protected as much as possible.

In this introductory chapter we look at how to prevent the molestation or abuse of children with special needs, including identifying some behavioral signs to look out for, and how to be proactive in stopping the molestation/abuse.

Preventing the molestation of children with special needs

While it is the ultimate responsibility of adults to keep all children safe, we also want children to be as independent as possible. Herein lies the dilemma. We simply cannot keep our eyes on our children 100 percent of the time, and so we must teach them appropriate behaviors. It is vitally important, for example, that children with special needs, no matter their ability to communicate, learn and become competent in the skill of self-advocacy to the highest degree possible. Many children with cognitive challenges or with autism spectrum disorders (ASD) have little or no language to express their thoughts or feelings. Other children may be hyper-verbal, but their comprehension or expressive skills are limited and not equivalent with their verbal skills.

We cannot assume that everyone in our family or in the schools or programs our child attends has her best interests at heart. Further, we cannot assume that if something untoward does happen, that she will be able to communicate that experience. It is especially important to develop alternative communication methods for the non-verbal child. In addition to programming an assistive technology/augmented communication device to help a child ask for a snack or to greet a family member, it is also important that all body parts are named, including the parts we consider private.

Very young children who may be typically developing or who have a special need do not understand the concept of germs, viruses, or bacteria, and do not comprehend that the spread of these things can make us sick. However, we spend a great deal of time reinforcing good hand washing practice. So, too, must we teach our children about the private nature of their genitalia, with the same amount of reinforcement accomplished by frequent education and calm, natural discussion. Put aside any resistance you may have about discussing specific genitalia and potentially harmful experiences your child may encounter. Helping your child to understand her body and when and how she should be treated can go a long way to keep her safe.

Normalizing the use of accurate words for genitalia, such as vagina and penis, are important to teaching children to protect themselves and, if need be, to accurately report molestation. Children who use augmentative communication devices have a section that contains body parts—just as we teach our children "nose" and "eye," so, too, must we teach them "vagina" and "penis." This education needs to continue, reinforcing the concept of private and appropriate touching. Giving a non-verbal child the ability to thwart unwanted and inappropriate interactions by others helps to keep her safe. In addition, giving her the tools to report any and all experiences can help you to understand what your child experiences in school or elsewhere.

Children with special needs must learn that just because a typical peer is behaving in a certain way, this is not always the correct way to be. With calm and clear repetition, most children can understand these subtleties. Helping a child to develop a sense of empowerment so that she can make her own decisions about what is right for her is also part of keeping her safe. Children with special needs require specific learning methods and accommodations so they may internalize the information and incorporate new and safe behaviors into their personal repertoires.

Although this may seem to be too complex or not appropriate for young children to learn, take note of the statistics. In 2010, statistics provided by the National Center for Victims of Crime reported that approximately 20 percent of girls and 5 percent of boys under the age of 13 have been sexually molested, with children with special needs three times as likely to be molested as their typically developing peers.

Understanding friendship and acts of kindness

According to Merriam Webster (2018), among other definitions, "friend" or "friendly" is described as "showing kindly interest and goodwill" and "not causing or likely to cause harm." Children are taught from a very early age that friendship is important and highly valued as they grow and develop. Children with special needs have particular difficulty defining "friendship" and what this means.

Non-verbal communication or body language

Children with special needs do not always understand the subtleties of non-verbal communication or body language. Often children trust the actions of others and take the behavior of others at face value. They do not interpret or look for a hidden agenda when someone is kind to them; they are simply pleased that someone is showing them attention. Children on the autism spectrum tend to have decreased eye contact. During conversations they may look away entirely or focus on the speaker's mouth or hands. Eyes often provide information about the speaker or actor's intention, so if children do not look directly at a person, or if they are not able to interpret the meaning of various facial expressions, they become vulnerable to malicious intent.

Non-verbal communication not only refers to body language; it also includes tone of voice, sarcasm, persuasive language, or hidden or double meanings. Children on the autism spectrum often have concrete thinking skills and do not look for hidden meaning or messages during a conversation or interaction, and it is this purity and innocence that creates a vulnerability that is often recognized and exploited by adults or children with ill intent.

The meaning of "friendship"

As a school occupational therapist I interact with many children with varying levels of cognitive and physical abilities. I have asked my students what it means to have a friend and they have often been unable to verbalize the answer. When I have asked how they know someone is their friend, they frequently use the word "nice." When someone is "nice" to them, they believe this person is a friend, and a friend, they understand, is a good thing. When asked to draw a picture of friends, they may draw a picture of two people holding hands or playing together. The children with special needs I work with go on to further explain that a friend is someone to share fun times.

Often my students explain to me that another adult is nice because they have given treats or small gifts to them. They understand these concrete interactions as expressions of kindness. While this is generally an accurate interpretation of the adult's behavior, at times this conduct is something else entirely. Children with special needs need to learn ways to recognize when someone is not being a true friend.

Molesters acting as "friends," using coercion and secrets

Herein lies the dilemma. Sadly, data show that most molesters are known to the child and family (National Center for Victims of Crime 2012), and often begin a relationship with a child by being "nice." These people often create fun times for the child, the victim. They may be present at family outings, holiday parties, or other events where there are many people and where parents' usual vigilance is weakened or diverted. They may even be family members. These people are kind to the child, perhaps even help the family, and may be well known to the family and familiar to the child for years before anything untoward occurs.

This close family member or friend may notice financial distress or childcare needs and will step up to help the family. He will then ingratiate himself into the family and may even become someone who is viewed as indispensable to the functioning of the household. This increased contact and involvement strengthens the bond between the family and the molester, who then becomes a trusted adult in the life of the family before the abuse begins. These relationships may be cultivated for years.

Often the child is encouraged to keep secrets from her parents before the molestation occurs. These secrets may start small and be innocent enough, such as the molester giving the child a piece of candy before dinner, or some other benign gift. The interaction between the molester and the child may be something like this: "We can stop at the ice cream shop before dinner, but don't tell your mom." In the case of the non-verbal child, the molester will gain the trust of the parents. When the parents are with the molester and the child, they observe an adult or older child taking good care of their child and showing love to the child and support (emotional or financial) to the family.

Soon the child becomes accustomed to keeping secrets from her parents and the bond between the child and molester strengthens. The child is used to keeping secrets about the relationship and interactions between herself and the abuser. When the abuse begins, slowly at first, the child keeps those interactions secret as well. The molester will then use his victim to help maintain the concealment of the abuse. As the molestation/abuse escalates, as it usually does, the child continues to keep the secret.

Many children who are victims of molestation/abuse are non-verbal or have limited expressive language. Children can express themselves in many other ways besides the use of language. For instance, a child's behavior is the key to her inner thoughts and wellbeing. Her behavior may change over time in ways that are not developmentally typical. Keep in mind that behavior is communication, and that it is the responsibility of the adults around the child to correctly interpret that behavior.

Behavioral signs of molestation/abuse

The behavioral changes listed in this section may or may not be signs of molestation/abuse. Children with special needs do, at times, exhibit a variety of changing behaviors for myriad reasons. The intention here is to increase awareness of behavioral changes that have been observed in children who have been victims of molestation/abuse. When other causes, such as illness or changes in a school setting or family situation have been ruled out, look further to understand what your child is working hard to communicate. Every situation is different, as is each child.

Increased anger or other mood changes

Your child may suddenly respond to an experience that in the past did not elicit an extreme reaction such as self-harm. She may hit herself or throw away a favorite toy. She may throw toys, furniture, or food, either randomly or directly at others. A child who in the past did not slap her face or genitals may begin to do so. She may lash out at beloved family members. Alternatively, she may become quiet. A previously outgoing or warm child may become shy and reserved during family times. She may resist any physical contact from relatives who have, in the past, greeted her with a hug. Your child may specifically resist interactions with either all the females or males she has had occasion to meet.

Loss of, or increased appetite

Your child may have a constant feeling of dread. She never knows when the molestation will occur and so she is in a state of high alert, constantly vigilant. Her body actually changes to "fight or flight" mode. If this happens, her nervous and circulatory systems change necessary bodily functions away from digestion and to the muscles. These basic, physical changes ready the body to escape or ward off danger. This happens involuntarily in response to the extreme and chronic stress caused by the molestation/abuse. If a child lacks the physical skill to move away, her body experiences the physiological changes in blood flow, respiration and so on associated with running away in fear. The child may be flooded with these metabolic changing hormones and has no way to release the stress caused by this state. The child is unable to overpower an adult, and so she becomes more and more confused and distressed as the abuse continues, in some cases for years.

Eating is one of few areas over which a child is able to exert control. If your child refuses to eat, or eats very little and this behavior is unusual, she may develop an eating disorder. This may be a direct result of being molested. The child feels as though she has no control over much of her life and her body, but eating is something she is able to control. Control in this area helps the child feel strong and somewhat in control, but it is not a healthy response to molestation/abuse, and may cause additional physical problems in the future.

Toileting accidents

Toilet accidents after toilet training has been accomplished are a common red flag to notice. The child who has been sexually molested will understandably feel uncomfortable in her genital area—the less time and attention spent on dealing with toileting issues, the less time the child needs to feel uncomfortable. If she is not using the toilet, she does not have to think about or touch her genitals. As a result, she will begin to wet herself again or even demonstrate encopresis. She may become resistant to having a bowel movement and develop stomach pains or become impacted. She may be having accidents or change her toileting habits as a way to exert some control over her body.

Touching of genitalia

Touching of genitalia on one's own body or others is another common occurrence that may be noticed by parents or caregivers as the result of a child having been molested. Some curiosity is a normal part of behavior; however, if the child is suddenly more interested than she had been in the past, further investigation into the cause of this behavior is appropriate. Increased interest in a child's own genitals may alert you to the onset of puberty. If this is the case, then teaching your child about the proper times and place to touch herself is important.

Unfortunately some children who have been sexually molested develop sexually transmitted diseases. If you notice any redness or sores in the genital area of your child, visit a healthcare provider as soon as possible.

Expressing an interest in touching genitalia

Expressing an interest in touching the genitalia of others (family members, classmates, or anyone she may come into contact with during the day) in a sexual manner should be concerning. The child may be re-enacting an experience she has had, and close attention should be paid to these interactions. She may express knowledge of sex acts or other behaviors that are considered adult—specific words or actions that are sexually implicit in nature are not normal behaviors in young children.

It is important to observe your child playing with her dolls and to listen to any narration she does during play. Overhearing and witnessing the words and actions she has with her toys is a good way to learn what your child is thinking and what she is experiencing when you are not present. While it is true that many children with an ASD engage in minimal imaginary play, they may at times use dolls and other representative toys to act out an experience they had or witnessed. It is important to pay attention to the way children use toys and listen to their words.

If a child overtly requests to touch your genitalia or for you or other family members to touch hers, this is not normal, and attention to these requests should be followed up with finding out where her ideas came from. Children on the autism spectrum have an uncanny ability to repeat verbatim complete conversations—do listen to what your child is saying. She may give you a great deal of information about what she has been experiencing.

Drawings of genitalia

A common assessment that is used with children is to request that they "draw a person." If the child is able, she is requested to draw a man, a woman, and then herself. Although not expressed in the directions, the expectation is that the person is drawn with clothing on. If the child draws the person naked, this is a significant cause for concern, and this is not normal for any child.

Exposing or examining one's own genitalia

While this is part of learning about oneself, excessive exposing behavior should be questioned. Teach your child at a level she will understand that the parts of the body covered by underwear are not to be seen or touched by other people.

If, for example, the child explicitly takes off her underwear and then directs her naked self to a male relative, this behavior needs to be addressed. Without an extreme reaction on your part, remove the child from the area and dress her immediately. In a calm manner, and in the way that you, as the parent, communicate with your child best, ask her to explain what she thinks she was doing and why she acted this way. Ask her, if at all possible, what sort of reaction she hoped to achieve, or how she came up with the idea to act this way. This may give you a good insight into what caused her to act this way. But be consistent—don't respond as though taking off her clothes is cute one day, and then be alarmed the next. Always calmly remove your child from the view of others, dress her, and simply state, "We keep our clothes on."

Increased or decreased interest in bathing

This is another reason to pay close attention to your child's behavior. Children with ASD and other special needs may have sensory processing challenges, and bathing is an area that is commonly difficult for a child with a sensory processing, tactile, auditory, or olfactory sensitivity. The child may be disturbed by the sound of the water, the temperature of the water, the feel of the cloth on her skin, the fragrance of the soap, having her head touched, or even the movement of the water in the bath tub.

These challenges do not appear suddenly. If the child suddenly acts as though she has a sensory processing challenge, pay attention and investigate the cause of this sudden change. The child who has experienced molestation may feel dirty and want to wash that feeling off. She may also feel uncomfortable about being naked and resist as much as possible having her clothing off, even during safe times at home. The feelings of fear and distrust stay with a child who is not able to discern different levels of safety in different settings. Once her trust has been broken, she may not feel safe with anyone at any time.

Unexplained opposition to be near certain people

Unexplained opposition to be with or near a specific family member or friend, when in the past your child was neutral about interacting with the individual, may be significant and should be questioned. Perhaps in the past she did not pay attention to the person or she may have even sought out this individual or appeared to enjoy interacting with him. If the relationship with a known adult or a child family friend or relative has suddenly changed without an obvious reason, make every attempt to have your child explain the reason for her sudden change of heart. If she is evasive or displays an extreme response, press on. Ask your child if that person has hurt her in any way. Assure your child that you will keep her safe, and if anyone is hurting her, you will put a stop to it. If your child is non-verbal, do not allow the person your child is resisting to be alone with her. This may be difficult if you have been depending on this person for childcare, but you need to trust your child and respect her feelings, even if you do not have concrete proof that anything wrong has occurred. If nothing else, you will be communicating to your child that you are paying attention to what she is communicating.

Resistance to attend events

Resistance to attend events when the child knows or assumes that the molester/abuser will also be in attendance is especially troublesome when this person is also a family member. Families with children with special needs depend on extended family to provide support and help with their child. If a child suddenly has tantrums or otherwise resists going to grandma's house, for example, because that is where the abuse has taken place or because she believes the abusive uncle may also be in attendance, it is important to listen to what the child is communicating. If she does not have the words to express her fears, it is vital that you stay very close to your child during the visit and assures her that nothing untoward will occur. Parental observation of a child's behavior is invaluable and cannot be substituted by the report of another adult.

Change in appearance

To appear unattractive as a means of discouraging a molester/abuser is another tactic a child may display. Children have control over very little. Like food choices and toilet habits, dressing may be another way for a child to have a bit of control in a world that otherwise feels out of control for her—clothing choices and grooming styles are ways we all express ourselves to the world. If your child suddenly expresses the desire to be dirty, smelly, disheveled, or otherwise purposely unattractive, she may, indeed, be going through a stage. She may also be acting this way as a defense. Children with higher cognitive understanding of cause and effect will use this tactic to prevent continued abuse/molestation.

If you observe this behavioral change, it is important that a frank conversation takes place. Using simple terms, ask your child if she is not bathing for a specific reason. Explain the consequences of not bathing on hygiene, health, and social participation. If she states that she is aware of these consequences and that is why she is choosing to maintain an unattractive physical state, explore further. Ask her if there is a specific person whose attention she is hoping to avoid.

Conversely, when the abusive "relationship" is beginning and the abuser is simply showing your child increased attention, she may respond by wanting to dress up or dress in a way that is older, more mature, or seductive than is appropriate for her age, such as pre-teen girls wearing clothing that is appropriate for older girls, or expressing an interest in wearing excessive makeup.

An otherwise outgoing child becoming withdrawn

An otherwise outgoing child may become withdrawn quite suddenly or over an extended time period. Your child may be feeling uncomfortable physically as well as emotionally. She will be distracted by confused feelings that she cannot express. Safety is a basic human need, and without feeling safe, survival is questioned and feels uncertain. A child with special needs may not be able to communicate these complex thoughts and feelings. She depends on her parents to help her express herself. She may need you to actually speak the words or help her to act out the abuse using dolls or drawings.

Decrease in school performance

Children, especially children with ASD, thrive when they have the opportunity to follow routines and procedures. All children learn best when they are able to participate in the classroom routine, and learning takes place when a child is engaged and feels safe. A child who is upset and/or distracted will not be able to follow a basic routine. If the teacher reports that a child's behavior has diminished in this area, this is cause for concern. Basic skills such as participation in the morning classroom procedures to start the day may become diminished when a child has experienced molestation/abuse. The child may suddenly need reminders about stowing her backpack or other arrival protocols.

If your child's grades suddenly take a downward turn, this is also a cause for concern, and you should try to understand the reason for this change. If your child is having difficulty with the specific subject matter, this is one reason for a downturn in grades, and could, perhaps, be resolved with tutoring. If, on the other hand, the teacher believes that your child should know the material being presented and cannot explain the reason for her poor academic performance, you will need to investigate further.

Apathetic behavior/loss of interest

Apathetic behavior/loss of interest in activities or recreational and leisure pursuits that in the past your child enthusiastically engaged in is certainly a red flag. What reason could there be for a child to suddenly lose interest in something fun? Try to ask your child to explain, in a manner that allows you to understand, her change of interest, if at all possible. It may be just that, a change of interest. Or it may be something more. Pay attention to the words and behaviors of your child. Give her time and let her know that whenever she is ready to let you know her thoughts and feelings, you are ready to listen.

If she does tell you that, in fact, abuse/molestation has taken place, try not to react with an intensity that will cause her to stop communicating with you. She will want to protect you from feeling upset. She will know that something wrong has occurred, but she may not have the words to explain her experience. She may feel embarrassed or she may feel shame. She may even believe that for some reason she caused the abuse to take place and that she is therefore a bad person.

Power imbalance

Children are taught to respect and believe adults simply because they are older. Molesters will often tell a child she is responsible for the sexual encounter. They may say that she "asked for it" or that she needs to do this for myriad reasons. Perhaps she was threatened to remain silent and keep the secret. She may believe that she is confiding in you at great risk to herself or others she loves. Children are at a power disadvantage. They are taught to respect adults, and adults are bigger and stronger. Communicate with your child so that she understands that her needs and safety are a top priority to you, and that you have the ability to keep her safe, no matter what any other person says.

Be proactive

Learning opportunities present themselves throughout the day. These opportunities occur organically as you move through various activities such as during bath time, shopping, going to parties or other outings with new or familiar people.

Take the time before each experience to reinforce the ideas of privacy and safety. After a social occasion, observe your child's behavior and responses when you review any experiences, good or bad, she may have had.

Learning opportunities during bath time

This is an excellent time to be proactive with teaching your child that her private parts are just that—private. During bath time, as your child gets older and more capable, delineate the parts of the body that are considered "private." Use the appropriate names for the body parts that are not to be touched by anyone else, except during medical or therapeutic times. During those accepted times, when your child will be without clothing or will be touched by a professional, give your child as much advance information as possible and be present with her during the examination or treatment. Teach your child the words: Vagina, Penis, Bottom, and Mouth/Tongue. These are all private parts and are not to be handled or touched by anyone else. Of course there are always exceptions, such as if your child is dependent for self-care skills and requires being fed or having a diaper changed.

As soon as your child has the physical functional hand skill, give her a washcloth and have her clean her private parts during bath time. This is a natural part of growing up, and it is very important that she becomes competent in this skill. Bath time is also a good time to practice the front to back motion used during toilet hygiene, which helps prevent infections.

Be aware of new friends

New friends are usually a cause for celebration, and it is possible that typically developing children befriend a child with special needs. When this happens it is a wonderful thing, with strong and mutual bonds developing and both parties benefiting greatly. But be aware of your child's new friends who may or may not have special needs. It is important to know how these friends are spending time with your child—it is okay to be a nosey parent, to know where she is going, her mode of transportation, who she will be with, and what activities she will be engaging in.

Do not allow your child to be alone with someone you do not know well, or who has suddenly entered your child's life. Enforce a rule that doors are to remain open at all times, and if at all possible, have the children play within your line of sight. You do not necessarily need to participate in the play activity, but you should know the nature of the play. Make a quick phone call to the parents of the new friend and get to know them. Check up on your child, while giving her room to grow and mature. This is a difficult balancing act, but a vital one for all parents. Make sure that your child's new friends are not exploiting her to perform sex acts or criminal behavior. Children with special needs want to have friends, and if an older or more sophisticated child promises friendship or a gift, a child with special needs may do just about anything to gain that connection.

Children with lower cognitive abilities than their typically developing peers may begin to feel lonely and isolated due to not being able to comprehend complex social interactions. Guide your child and her new friends by providing simple activities that they can all enjoy, such as simple bead stringing to make necklaces or baking or other simple food preparations.

Be aware of an increase in somatic complaints or night terrors

Sometimes children use the "stomach ache" complaint to stay home from school. This is a natural school avoidance technique that has been used for ages. Children may also complain of headaches, stomach aches, strained limbs, or fatigue. If this happens once, or rarely, it is certainly not cause for concern. If such somatic complaints become common and varied, pay attention to what your child is saying. Ask yourself what she is trying to avoid. These complaints may actually indicate a medical condition, but if a medical condition is ruled out, probe until you fully understand the reason for her avoidance behavior.

A child may also have nightmares or night terrors. A child who has had no difficulty in the past sleeping all through the night may suddenly wake up with bad dreams. She may begin to wet the bed or refuse to have the lights off. Honor your child's fears. She is communicating something and it is up to you to interpret that communication. If these fears persist, help your child to express the cause of this behavior. Assure her that you have the skill and power to take care of and eliminate the cause of her worries. Your child cannot hear too many times that she is your number one priority, and you want her always to feel safe and happy.

Children depend on parents and teachers to keep them safe. If a responsible adult in a child's life notices any of the above behavioral changes, it is extremely important that the issue be addressed as soon as possible.

Be aware of who is communicating with your child

Children with special needs have a difficult time being heard and understood, and changes in behavior may be explained away as a stage or acceptance that the child is "difficult." All behavior communicates the state of inner being of any person, so it is vitally important that the child is believed, especially the non-verbal child who is expressing herself with a change in behavior.

While surveillance technology exists that would allow you to view your child in almost any setting, it is not in use in many schools, so you need to be extra vigilant, especially with a child with special needs who is non-verbal or who is not able to accurately recount any experience due to delayed expressive language skills.

Children who do not have typical cognitive development often have difficulty with spatial and temporal concepts—they are not able to report experiences, even if they are happy times, with accuracy, about time and place. Be aware that although a child tells you about something that occurred at school "yesterday," she may actually mean last week or another time. The accuracy of the specific time of the report by your child is not relevant when she is sharing an experience. What is most important and relevant is the nature of her experience and how that experience makes her feel.

Be aware of who interacts with your child

There are many staff personnel (childcare aides, teacher's aides, bus drivers and monitors, Sunday school teachers, coaches, clergy, and so on) in every child's life on a regular basis. Knowing every adult who comes into contact with your child may be difficult to achieve, but it is necessary. When you enroll your child in a school or other program, make the requirement known to school administrators that you want to have the names of everyone your child interacts with. This proactive approach may prevent misunderstanding in the future. Also explain that you would like to be made aware of any staff change in the class. If, for example, there is a substitute teacher or aide, let the administration know that you would like to be informed of this substitute as soon as the sub is scheduled. Make sure to provide the school or other administrative staff with updated and reliable contact information. If the administration balks at having to inform you, calmly explain to them that it is within your parental rights to know who is interacting with your child. Some parents find it helpful to have a daily email from the teacher or other primary caregiver or educator who is with your child. If technology is not appropriate, a simple notebook can travel back and forth from home to school as a daily communication log.

In addition to the academic and other school activities your child may have been participating in during the day, request a list of the adults who also interacted with your child. The easiest way to do this is to have the teachers fill in and recount your child's experiences, perhaps by the hour. This sort of ongoing communication is often used when a child exhibits a behavioral problem and time periods are used as an opportunity for reward intervals. Most teachers will be familiar with this sort of log. Simply ask them to jot down the names and positions of the adults who interacted with your child and what specifically was done, on the same sort of time interval log. Hopefully this will be a routine exercise for the teacher as well as for you, the parent. You will learn how your child spends her day, and you can review this information as part of an evening routine.

If you notice any new adults listed on the log or your child displays unusual behaviors or responses during a specific time of day or at the mention of someone's name, investigate further. Your child may not have the ability to let you know why she is responding the way she did, so it is up to you to then question the teacher. If the teacher is evasive or otherwise resistant to discuss the issue you have, and you believe your child is not being treated well at school, it is within your rights to take the issue up the chain of command and to seek a supervisor's involvement. Remember that your child is the consumer in this scenario, and the reason the staff have employment is because your child participates in that specific school or program. You have every right to have your questions answered to the fullest extent you desire.

If your child is living in a residential setting, it is especially important to know the staff. Make it a point to visit at inconsistent times without prior notice. If the staff believe that you or other family members or friends may come by at any time, they are more likely to have your child appropriately cared for and her environment and belongings in good condition at all times. This is a sad commentary, but observation does impact behavior.

Be aware of who has augmented interest in your child

Many parents are over-burdened with work, transportation, medical appointments, therapy, and often other children in the family. Some parents work more than one job and days are filled with complicated schedules for each member of the family. The daily list of family commitments is almost endless.

If another adult becomes very helpful, almost indispensable to the running of the household, the motivation of this person may be pure, or it may not. Notice an augmented interest by an adult or older child who may or may not be a family member (increased offers of childcare or transportation, for example). Often a molester/abuser will take his time ingratiating himself to the family.

Pay attention to the behavior and demeanor of your child after this individual has increased his involvement with your family. Look for any of the behavioral signs listed above. If you do not know a coach (for example) well, do not accept the offer of a ride for your child. If you do know the adult well, and this offer appears to be out of the ordinary, politely defer. If the person insists or otherwise acts in an unusually persistent way about spending time alone with your child, even if it is "only" to give her a ride home, you most likely have made the correct decision to limit his involvement with your child. Many organizations now prohibit one adult to be alone with a child or groups of children. Learn what the supervision guidelines are for activities your child may participate in, such as sports or Scouts.

Take time to listen to your child report about her experiences when you are not with her

Ask questions about your child's experiences when she was not in your care. These questions may be ordinary ones, such as asking about what she did, who was there, and so on. If your child is verbal and seems to be evasive, don't let that pass. Listen carefully to what she is NOT saying. Ask the question a variety of ways, and always believe what your child is saying.

Pay attention to any gaps in time. If your child consistently omits information about, for example, the first 30 minutes of her dance lesson, investigate the reason for this. Open-ended questions are best. For example, "When you arrived at that dance studio, what did you do?" instead of asking, "Did you put on your outfit first?" Asking specific questions is not generally a problem, but if you want to get information about something that you have no knowledge of or cannot imagine, it's best to leave the option open for your child to say whatever is on her mind. You don't know what you don't know. If you are asking about her dance outfit, she may think that this is the only thing you have an interest in rather than something else that may be of concern to her.

Helping your child to communicate with you as accurately as possible about her experience is another reason to use the correct terminology when discussing body parts. Using euphemisms causes a greater chance of miscommunication, and you may not hear or understand important information your child is trying to have you know.

If your child is non-verbal, review the communication log you have established with her teacher. Using picture icons or other communication techniques, review the day with your child as much as possible. This is helpful in many ways. Your child will know that you have an interest in how she spends her time when you are not around. You will become aware of any changes in routines or staff. This will help you to be alert to any questionable experiences your child may have had.

Encourage your child to draw pictures of the times when she is not in your care, and then ask her open-ended questions about the pictures, such as, "Can you tell me about this?" or "What is happening here?" Invite your child to replay an interaction she has had either at school or in some other setting. Allow your child to use her dolls and to direct the play. Ask her who she would like you to be and how you should act.

What to do if you suspect molestation/abuse

If you do discover that your child has been touched inappropriately, assure your child that she is not to blame. Reinforce and repeat the concept to your child that you are on her side and you believe her, above anyone else. Contact the legal authorities as soon as possible. It is a good idea to let your child know that the perpetrator will no longer be allowed near her and you will keep her safe. Repeat this fact often, as this child needs a lot of reassurance and comfort.

Don't keep it a secret

Share your concerns with other adults you trust. Try to find out if other families have had similar suspicions or experiences with their own children. If the abuse is happening within a family, it is important to acknowledge the feelings of betrayal and the complex ties that exist. Above all, keep your priorities clear. You are most interested in protecting your child and getting her the professional help she needs. Family members may turn on you and accuse you of causing harm to a beloved uncle, for example. This is unfortunate, but your priority is your child and other children in the family.

Do everything within your power to stop the molestation from continuing. Report your suspicions to the agencies in your area that are charged with protecting children. Get your child the help she needs and deserves. You can find some resources for help listed at the back of this book.

Listen to your little voice inside

Let your maternal or paternal instinct come through to protect your child. If there is someone interacting with your child who makes you feel uncomfortable, honor yourself. Do not allow social convention or polite behavioral standards to inhibit you from protecting your child. Ask yourself why you feel this way. Try to find out as much as you can about the person who is making your feel uncomfortable. Do not doubt yourself. Intuition uses subconscious mechanisms to provide information that may not otherwise be obvious. You do not need to have empirical evidence or to witness an encounter. If something is making you feel uncomfortable, respect that feeling. It is not important to always walk through the world explaining yourself to others. You know what is best for your child and you have every right to act on that knowledge.

Keep your child and yourself safe

If you fear any danger at all from the abuser, do not approach him directly. Do everything you can to avoid contact with the person and let law enforcement help you and your child to stay safe. Enlist other trusted adults in the pursuit of maintaining the safety of all children. Change your location if need be by going to the home of a trusted friend or a shelter in your area.

Contact the law

No matter who you suspect, call the local law enforcement. The law varies depending on your residential location. Civilized society has no tolerance for adults who harm children, especially vulnerable children with special needs who have little capacity to protect themselves. You are within your rights to contact law enforcement even if you have a suspicion and do not have concrete evidence. You are not an investigator. Calmly explain your suspicions to the authorities; they are the ones tasked with uncovering the specifics of the circumstances.

Become familiar with school policy

Request information about the protocols of supervision at your child's school, specifically the ratio of students to adults at all times. The classroom, during instructional time, may have a good ratio of one teacher to four students or even one to three. This sounds like a reasonable ratio for children needing supervision and the provision of directed learning experiences.

Ask what the supervision ratio is during recess time and in the lunch room. It is also important to know what the use of the toilet policy is and the standards across the school, or if these protocols are left to the discretion of each individual teacher. If your child is independent with using the toilet, ask where the rest room is located in relation to your child's classroom. Make yourself familiar with the layout of the school. If the children in the class have the option of using a toilet that is located within the classroom, there is most likely only space for one student at a time in the room. If, however, the toilet is in the hallway, it is most probable that there are multiple stalls.

As children with special needs need clear and consistent rules, make it clear that your child is to use the toilet alone. She does not need a friend to accompany her to the toilet; this is not a time to socialize. Rather, it is time to take care of a personal need and return to class as quickly as possible.

Security cameras are becoming more and more common in many places. Request that they are set up so that the entrances to the rest rooms are monitored. Have the use of these security measures well known to everyone in the school. Often the awareness of the possibility of being observed is a deterrent to potential molesters.

Understand the pass policy of your child's class by getting answers to the following questions:

- Is there a time limit for the use of the pass?

- Can more than one student leave the room at the same time?

- What are the reasons for a child to be given the pass to leave the room? What errands necessitate the child taking a pass to leave class? If one of the reasons is to return a book to the library, why can this not happen during specifically designated library time? What are all the scenarios during the school day that would necessitate your child leaving the classroom without an adult to supervise and escort her?

Use of this book

The following chapters provide lessons and guidelines for activities that may be used in either educational or home settings. Every attempt has been made to provide an easily modifiable curriculum so that the widest spectrum of developmental levels will be able to benefit.

Those familiar with the ADOS-2 (Autism Diagnostic Observation Scale-2; see Western Psychological Services 2012) will notice some correlation with the structure of this test in that activities have been developed for non-verbal and minimally verbal children as well as children with fluent speech.

It is my sincere hope that this book will give caring adults information and empowerment to prevent children with special needs from having to endure potential molestation/abuse. There are estimates that one in five girls and one in twenty boys are victims of abuse or molestation, and further exploration of this topic reports that children with special needs are three times more likely to be victimized than their typically developing peers (National Center for Victims of Crime 2012).

— CHAPTER 2 —

Friendship

What is friendship?

According to Alice Walker, "No person is your friend who demands your silence, or denies your right to grow." Friendship is an elusive concept, albeit an experience all people crave. Without words to define the concept of friendship it is a feeling that is universal. We know when someone is our friend, but how do we know this? How do children with special needs understand friendship? How do they know when someone is being a friend? How do we teach them when someone is not being a friend? And how can they tell the difference?

In this chapter, my intention is to help you to begin to think about the issue of friendship in relation to the children with special needs in your life. Acknowledging that there may be people in your life and in the life of your child who appear to be friends, but in reality who are not, is a difficult idea to come to terms with. We do not want to accept the fact that our child may be being molested by someone we call a friend or even a dear family member, but unfortunately the statistics are not in favor of family and friends—most abuse or sexual molestation is perpetrated by close family members or friends.

Learning social skills

Friendship is valued highly and seen as a goal to aspire towards. When children with special needs have a friend, someone to play with after school, or someone who invites them to a party, it is a source of pride for parents—having a friend is seen as a great accomplishment, and rightly so. Children with special needs, no matter the nature of their functional skills, have every right to feel the warmth and companionship that friendship brings. All lives are enhanced by the acceptance and shared experiences with a loving friend.

Friendship can be based on shared experiences and interests. It can also be based on mutual respect. Often, in school, friendships develop when children see each other daily and become familiar with each other. They have common experiences and shared interests.

As parents and others who care deeply about our children's happiness, we want them to have friends. Friends represent a full life. For children along the spectrum of special needs, however, friendship is a very sensitive and often difficult issue, and children with special needs require help to develop relationships. We want our children to behave in ways that encourage bonds between them and other children. We hope that other parents will see our children as good playmates and want our children to enjoy being together. Planning play dates is a common way to foster friendships among children of any ability level.

Children with an ASD often find themselves in a group in school or in an after-school program that provides "social skills training" (Baker 2003). This is popular and often focuses on friendship, and on how children with special needs can and should behave; in fact, they are often told that they should behave in specific ways in order to develop friendships. Children are taught to defer to the interests of others and to participate in activities that may not be of interest so that others will want to be in their company and become their "friend." This may set them up for becoming accustomed to feeling uncomfortable for the sake of having a friend.

Social skills training programs rarely address the idea that having friends is not the most important part of childhood, above all else. Given the choice between being safe and having a friend, being safe is the better alternative, but this idea is overlooked in most lessons about friendship. A child with special needs can, at times, appear lonely, and may find herself suddenly being invited to join a group of other schoolmates who appear popular; this group may or may not have healthy reasons for including the child with special needs. Perhaps the other students are truly being kind, or perhaps they have other, less healthy or positive reasons for giving attention to this child.

When typically developing students decide to exploit or otherwise harass or abuse another child, especially a child with special needs who believes that these children are acting out of friendship, the group or individual may smile and cheer her on as a way to encourage her to act in a silly way so that others laugh at her. She may be encouraged to show her private parts or touch other children's private parts or even to act out sexually, all the while being assured that this is the way the popular kids are acting.

In some instances, another child who also has special needs may molest or otherwise harm another child. When this occurs, the child may not even understand that what she has participated in is wrong. She may, in fact, be acting out abuse or molestation that she herself has experienced.

It is important for the child with special needs to know that this is not the price of friendship. Real friendship does not ask another person to compromise her safety or violate her in any way. The child with special needs may not understand the subtle communication between the individuals in the popular group. Increasing her skill set to include recognition of when she is being treated poorly, and learning how to respond in these situations, is an important way to help your child who is vulnerable to stay safe. (Non-verbal communication skills are discussed in the following chapter.)

Learning personal boundaries

Frank and open discussions about personal boundaries are important and a good starting place for educating your child on the issue of the good behavior of others towards her. These should happen as young as possible—certainly by age three or earlier. Just as you start teaching your child that hand washing is an important skill to keep her safe and healthy, so, too, is the practice of protecting her by her being aware of knowing and understanding her own personal boundaries.

Teaching children that a friend would not cross personal boundaries or coerce another to cross those boundaries is an important lesson that needs to be learned. The child who has a strong sense of self in terms of personal space can prevent others from violating that space. The earlier the child learns this lesson, the stronger the lesson is, and the more firmly it becomes part of her.

Children of all ability levels are great observers and imitators. As parents we are often surprised to hear words or observe actions by our children that we had no idea that the child had learned. Sometimes we are embarrassed because we had not realized that our child knew a specific word, such as an expletive blurted out when we stub our toe, which may be repeated by our child at a most inopportune moment. So, too, are our actions observed, learned, and repeated by children. Demonstrating our own personal boundaries in our daily life is a great learning tool for our children. Think of interactions with other people that may require the exertion of personal boundaries, such as trying on clothing in a store. With your child with you in the dressing room, show clearly that you are closing the door so that you may have privacy. If you are at the library and a stranger approaches your child or stands too close to you or your child for your comfort as he speaks with you, take a step back and simply state, we can talk from here, or we can sit across the table from a person and not next to him. There are myriad examples in daily life that you can think of once you turn your attention to this concept.

As with all learning, a multifaceted approach allows information to be absorbed with more influence. All children learn in different ways, and the same child needs different modalities to learn different information, so the more varied the methods used to present a single concept, the more likely your child will learn the behaviors she needs to keep herself safe.

When you have a quiet moment with your child, pay attention to having her learn about her own personal space and physical boundaries. This should be done frequently, perhaps on a weekly basis—if not more often—when a situation arises, as in the bath tub, for example. Here are some activities you can use to reinforce the concept of personal boundaries with your child of any developmental level, followed by some simple rules. These may be used with verbal and non-verbal children as well as with children who have full physical capabilities or who may have motor limitations—as always, you know your child best and the best ways to adapt activities and materials for her specific needs.

Activities to learn personal boundaries

- Place a small towel or blanket on the floor. Place a puzzle or another toy with multiple pieces on the blanket and show your child that this is the only space for these toys—they are to remain within this space. Pretend that other toys want to "invade" the space of that particular puzzle, and pretend that one of the puzzle pieces is saying, "No! This is my space alone." Have the other toy move away, back to its own bin or perhaps onto another towel, where it belongs.

You could also ask your child to separate the pieces of a toy or game that don't match or that don't belong with the ones you have identified as belonging in that space.

- Wrap a towel or blanket around your child, and say or show her that this is her space and others are not to enter her space without her permission. (It is important to explain to other family members who rush to hug your child that you are teaching her about personal boundaries, and while you know that hugging is a wonderful way to express affection, ask them if they will please ask permission before giving your child a hug or a kiss on the cheek. Your child should never be forced to accept affection from anyone.)

- Act out the above scenario with favorite dolls or puppets. Have one doll want to give her friend a hug, and have the other put her arms out and say something in the nature of "Not now" or "Let's just shake hands and play with these blocks together." Keep the scene as simple as possible with an emphasis on one doll saying, "No" and the other doll accepting this response.

- Have your child draw a picture of people (most children enjoy drawing family members). Draw a circle around yourself in the picture. Encourage your child to draw a picture around her and the others as well. Explain to your child, "This is your personal bubble," outline the circle with your finger in the picture, then in the air surrounding your child, simply state, "No one gets into your bubble without you saying that it is okay."

- Using dolls or puppets, demonstrate personal space—have the dolls or puppets ask permission of each other to enter the other's personal space and interact.

Simple rules

- Private parts (those covered by underwear or a bathing suit) and the mouth are considered private, and these body parts are not to be touched by a friend—ever.

- Do not to touch the private parts area of another person, even if he has clothing on, no matter how kindly he asks, and even if he offers a treat or other prize.

- Do not take off clothing in school or anyplace else without your parent's permission.

- Someone should not be allowed to take off your clothing. (Of course there are exceptions, such as when a child needs to be changed due to an "accident" in school. We are not going to confuse children with these nuances here; they need to learn that taking clothing off during playtime with a friend never happens at all.)

- Do not look at the private parts of another person—if someone wants to show you a private part, run away and tell an adult.

- Do not look at pictures of private parts or of people showing private parts or touching each other.

- Do not watch another person touch his or her own private parts.

- Do not watch two other people touch the private parts of each other.

- Do not allow someone to take a picture of you. (Of course another exception comes up, especially in the school setting when pictures are used for yearbooks and other fun creations. Make sure, as a parent, you are made aware of the possibility of your child being photographed and sign permission for this to occur. Read the document carefully so you know precisely how the photos will be used.)

- Do not let another person touch your backpack or take things out for you.

- Do not let another person touch your lunch, or eat your lunch.

- A good friend respects her own boundaries and others' boundaries.

Of course there are exceptions and subtleties with all human behavior. Children with special needs need to learn the concrete skill first, then, over time, they can learn when exceptions are allowed. One such exception to the rule about taking off clothing, for example, is at bath time and bed time. Your child will learn through repetition that these are acceptable times to remove clothing and who the people are who may help with this self-care routine. As soon as your child is able to wash her own private parts, allow her to do so. Turn away so that she understands that this is a private activity and that she is responsible for taking care of herself.

Learning what to do when others are not acting as a friend

Children in a social skills group may learn how to treat others, but will not extrapolate that behavior in the reverse—they will not understand that others need to act in particular ways towards them as well. Rarely, if ever, are children taught that they need to notice and accept the fact that another child or adult is not treating them well.

It is important not to take it for granted that a child with special needs will know when another is not treating her well, or that another child is a negative rather than a good influence. I have seen this many times in my work as a school occupational therapist. Often a child with a cognitive delay will not understand the nature of the behavior of another child or adult, and so, when outrageous and disruptive behavior is witnessed, it will be imitated. The louder and more outrageous the behavior, the more likely other child with special needs will copy the inappropriate actions. The child may even seek out the outrageous actor to cultivate a friendship.

It is important for children to be able to differentiate between a dangerous behavior and one that is simply not to their liking. This is the reason that adult supervision is crucial in keeping children safe.

It may be difficult, but children need to be taught to discern if participation in a non-preferred activity is in their best interests or not. With adult supervision and encouragement, children with a rigid sense of likes and dislikes may discover new interests or activities they enjoy if they are open to the experience. A trusted adult can help teach this distinction to children.

They also need to learn that at times it is okay to put their own needs and interests first, as a priority. Each situation should be addressed individually, as generalization is difficult and should not be assumed, especially in children with an ASD.

At times the answer will be "No!" A child should feel free to say "No" when another child touches her in her private parts or asks to see her private parts. A child should feel free to say "No" when she is asked to touch, lick, fondle, suck, or otherwise handle the private parts of another child or adult.

Children with special needs do not generalize information. While a child with special needs may do well in a group setting with a leader teaching the skill of sharing toys, for example, or during a role-playing exercise, and may even demonstrate sharing when asked to perform this behavior in a structured learning environment, when she leaves the group, she will not necessarily understand that the skill she just learned and demonstrated is something to be used in other settings as well.

Children with special needs *can* learn these skills and behaviors to be safe; they just need more time, repetition, and attention to their unique learning styles. Presenting information in a variety of methods and different locales reinforces the information and helps children integrate the information and behaviors so that their own personal safety becomes part of a natural response to uncomfortable and even dangerous contacts. Different ways to present information include verbally (storytelling), with pictures or with dolls, and physically moving dolls to act in specific ways. It is most helpful if your child is involved with the actions or drawings.

Friendship should not be used as a weapon or to coerce another person to participate or act in a certain manner. Often a child with a low cognitive level will be influenced to participate in an undertaking by the other person saying something in the nature of, "I thought you were my friend. If you are my friend, then kiss my penis." The power of having a friend and wanting to please a friend and be accepted by that friend cannot be underestimated.

Good examples and positive environments

Current educational practice emphasizes cooperative learning and the inclusion of children with special needs into the general education setting. While there are many reasons that children with special needs benefit from interaction and the behavior modeling of typically developing children, these settings may also mean less supervision and possibly more interaction with a greater variety of children and adults.

As the parent of a child with special needs, you will want to make sure that the other children your child is interacting with are behaving in a way that is acceptable to you. Inform the school that you would like to observe the general education class that your child will be entering, as you want to see how the other children act during instructional time, as well as during lunch and recess. When you first enter a school you can get a sense of the culture that exists. Listen to how the adults speak with each other and to the general sounds within the school. Observe the overall environment to see if it is a cheerful and creative place, or dark, cluttered or otherwise unpleasant.

Observing children play without a specific structure or the direct supervision that is provided within the classroom can provide information about the nature of the setting your child will experience:

- When you first enter the school office, are you greeted warmly? Every school has a culture and community unique to itself. Tune in to how you feel when you enter the school and the specific classes that your child will join.

- Does the school have an overall sense of community or does each class have its own individual identity and set of standards for appropriate behavior? Pay attention to how the teacher interacts with the students.

Are classmates encouraged to interact with each other in a cooperative and helpful manner?

- Is there an overall behavioral philosophy that everyone in the school is aware of and follows? Does the school have reinforcement strategies in place to encourage good citizenship?

- Are there realistic expectations for behavior, and rewards and consequences that are consistently adhered to by all teachers and staff? Do different children need to abide by different standards based on ability levels, or is everyone expected to meet the same benchmark?

- Are the staff members who are assigned to the play area during recess visible and available for the students, or are they off to the side speaking with each other or on their smartphones?

- Are the staff encouraging or yelling at the children? Are the educational staff or para-professionals who are assigned to the play area skilled in resolving spats between children? Do they encourage the children to resolve differences, or do they take over and resolve disputes with power?

- Who is the leader of the group of children, the one who is creating the rules and telling the other students what their roles are?

- Are the children sharing equipment or are some being discouraged from playing with the group (is there bullying)?

- What is the noise level? Many children with special needs have auditory sensitivity, and accommodations may be needed if your child is to be successful in a rambunctious play setting.

- Are the children using playground and other equipment safely and as intended?

- Are there any hidden areas in the class, the hallway, or outside? (These may present opportunities for molestation/abuse to occur.)

- Is the equipment safe and in good repair?

- Do all the children seem happy and friendly, or are they tense?

- Do the children include everyone in their games or are some wandering around the periphery of the play area or sitting alone?

- In general, are the children kind and caring towards each other?

The child who acts in a loud and disruptive manner in class will provoke a response from the teacher—only the most talented teacher can ignore disruptive behavior and respond to that behavior without interrupting the rest of the students and the learning process. Even if the teacher uses the best practice of minimizing the disruption, the other students are aware of what is happening in the class. And children always learn from each other.

No matter the response of the teacher, some attention has inevitably been paid to the child behaving negatively. The child with special needs does not necessarily understand the differences between positive and negative attention—all attention is reinforcing. She may then mimic or respond to the negative behavior that has been modeled, and learn that this way of acting is a way to get attention from the teacher. Another response may be for the child with special needs to quietly observe and develop a respect and admiration for the child who is getting attention from the teacher. She may not actually act out in the negative way the other student is, but may want to become a friend to that student.

A child may be attracted to a disruptive or otherwise "naughty" child who is not setting a good example to the child with special needs. The child with special needs does not discern the difference between positive or negative attention received by her classmate. Often disruptive behavior in a classroom will illicit giggles or other encouragement from peers. The student who was disruptive will see this as an opportunity to take advantage of another child who does not understand that this was bad behavior. The badly behaved student may encourage the child who is weaker or has an intellectual disability to also act in a way that is disruptive and interrupt the learning process for her as well as for the other students.

Students with negative behavior have their own reasons for acting inappropriately, and when the child with special needs gives them attention, this feels good, reinforcing the negative behavior—the offer of friendship from this poor behavior model is one that the child with special needs will find difficult to resist.

Learning "right from wrong" is a simple platitude, but it is vital that the specifics of what is the right behavior and kind of friends to pursue is a lesson that children need to learn. Use examples and experiences your child has on a daily basis to help decide with your child who would be a good friend for her to have, and who would not.

Learning about when and when not to keep secrets

Your child may wonder if all her friends will insist that she keep a secret about things that cause her to feel bad. Or perhaps she may be threatened if she tells anyone what has transpired. She may wonder if all friends eventually become dangerous and frightening powerful people who can harm the ones she loves.

Nuances and exceptions are difficult for children with special needs to comprehend. Children with an ASD resist deviations, and will often act out if there is a change in routine or circumstances. This is one of many times when this characteristic is helpful and can be used to the child's advantage. This adherence to rules should be encouraged and can help keep your child safe.

It is best to have a concrete rule about secrets, and that rule is simple: DO NOT KEEP SECRETS FROM YOUR PARENTS. Nothing that happens at school or sports practice or Scouts or church needs to be a secret from parents. Nothing that happens at the grandparents' home or indeed any place where the parents are not present should be kept secret. Secrets are unhealthy and often dangerous.

A predatory molester/abuser will often enlist the good nature of a child with special needs to keep a secret. This child may feel empowered or important when this other older child or adult, and perhaps someone she admires, is asking for her help with keeping a secret. The secret may begin innocently with a benign experience such as an extra snack before dinner. Once the child is in the habit of keeping a secret with this person from her parents, she is more likely to keep other interactions with the person a secret. And when molestation or abuse occurs, the child will naturally fall into the behavior of keeping that a secret as well. The child has been trained, through the repetition of keeping secrets, to keep this horrible secret as well.

When it is clear in your mind as a parent that no secrets are to be kept from you by your child, you will then be able to clearly communicate this idea to your child. No means no! Words are important. It is very important, especially with children on the autism spectrum, to use consistent language and mean what is said. For example, children enjoy making surprise gifts for parents. These should be referred to as "surprises" or "specials," not "secrets." Just as we don't call medicine "candy" when we are encouraging our child to take a needed medication, it is important to be clear and concrete. Surprises are just that, but secrets are not to be kept.

Some social skills training teaches children that if a friend asks them to keep a secret, then being a good keeper of secrets means being a good friend. Typically developing children will understand that a secret about a personal family matter is different than a secret about something dangerous. For example, if one child tells another that her parents are getting a divorce, but does not want others to know, that is a personal secret. If, on the other hand, one child exposes himself to another, or asks another child to touch his penis and to keep this a secret, this is a dangerous secret and should not be kept a secret. Children with special needs will not understand this difference and should never be put in the situation that requires them to discern the difference.

There are subtle differences in the nuances of interpersonal behavior and communication, and these ideas are difficult for children with special needs to understand. What kinds of secrets are safe to keep? When should the child betray trust and tell a secret? What about children who are non-verbal and who do not have the ability to use assistive technology to communicate? How should an assistive technology device be programmed to address secrets and inappropriate behavior? Speak with the therapist who is working with your child and her assistive technology, and request some icons that refer to feelings of safety, not just happy or sad.

Skills for making friends and being a friend

It is important to teach your child how to be a good friend, and it is equally important to help her understand how to know when someone is being a true friend to her. The following activities were developed to act as a guide to help you communicate with your child with special needs and to facilitate an understanding of the reciprocal nature of friendship in a way your child will understand.

The activities have been separated by developmental and skill level of children. Just as children do not fit neatly into one box, so, too, these activities are to be used only as a guide and may be used by children with different skill levels than the heading suggests. For example, do not skip over the activities recommended for a non-verbal child if your child is a chatterbox. You know your child best and so you decide the best way to interact with her.

Rarely are children taught how to recognize if someone is being a true friend to them or how to know if others are not being friends. The emphasis seems to be a bit one-sided. Later in this chapter we discuss the difficult concept of understanding when another person may appear to be a friend, but who, in reality, is not.

Lessons that teach important skills need to be repeated in a variety of ways so the information is integrated and becomes a natural part of the child's repertoire of responses, so that the child is able to fully understand what is being taught. Some of the different ways to teach these complex and often difficult concepts are through:

- Stories

- Drawings

- Role-playing

- Playing with dolls

- Frank conversations

- Using icons or symbols—pictures or three-dimensional items

- Practice during pretend play

- Modeling

- Helping your child to "notice" other people acting well.

Think about the child who is not able to read but who is able to recognize a fast food logo. She has seen that logo hundreds, if not thousands, of times. We are certain she is able to recognize that logo; she has learned that lesson well. So, too, will a child learn the lesson of keeping herself safe with repetition and with the information presented in a variety of settings. Remember, also, that learning takes place best when your child is relaxed and having fun.

The following activities are for non-verbal or minimally verbal children.

Activities for sharing

Perhaps your child has some favorite dolls or puppets or other character toys that are suitable to use when acting out an interactive scene. Create a simple scenario for the dolls and show your child how the dolls are kind to each other. Perhaps they are sharing toys or a treat. Have one of the dolls overtly take more than her fair share. With a sad face and unhappy icon or the simple statement "Not a good friend," communicate with your child that this doll is not being a good friend.

Activities for helping

Often children are taught that helping another person is a good way to be a friend. In this scene have the dolls help each other lift a heavy object together or clean up a messy space. Perhaps the dolls were painting together and now it is time to clean up—the dolls help each other. One doll pretends to help, but really allows the other to do all the work. This is not being a good friend. Using the same communication method as above, let your child know, that just because another is near her, he is not being a good friend if he is not doing his fair share.

As your child is engaged in this pretend play, have one doll that is at first acting like a friend, and then ask this doll friend to touch his private parts or try to touch the other doll. Have the second doll push away the offender's hand and leave the area. Have the doll communicate that she knows this is not how friends treat each other.

Activities to show encouragement

Children who are supported by peers feel empowered to do their best. Good friends encourage others to try new things and put effort into their endeavors so they can reach their potential. Have the dolls encourage each other during play. Perhaps they are excited about building a tall tower of blocks or fully coloring in a picture. Choose an activity that you know your child will understand. Choose something with which she has had some experience. After the dolls play for a while, have the naughty doll encourage the other doll to do something that is not good. Perhaps she wants to color on the walls or jump off of the high tower that they built. Have the one doll encourage the other doll to participate in the negative behavior. Choose a scenario that is realistic in your child's experience and one that she will understand to be dangerous or wrong. Again, using the form of communication that your child understands best, let her know that the doll, although encouraging and outwardly pleasant to the other doll, is not being a good friend.

Activities to demonstrate turn taking

Taking turns at using a favorite toy or sitting in a special spot is a skill we hope our children learn. At times, however, adults or even other children may use this technique to entice a child with special needs to engage in behavior that is dangerous, illegal, or increases the possibility of her being molested or abused. Turn taking is not appropriate in the case of, "I'll show you mine, then you show me yours," or "I'll try this [drugs or alcohol], then you have some too."

During this activity have the doll demure when encouraged to perform an act that may be dangerous. Using the simple statement "No, you first" communicates the preference of the doll to have the doll with the idea demonstrate the act. If the first doll refuses, the second doll knows that she does not want to perform the act either. Even if the first doll does act in a dangerous manner, have the second doll continue to refuse.

Children with special needs sometimes fall victim to other children who think it funny to encourage them to act in a way that is dangerous or embarrassing. The child with special needs may not understand that the other child is not smiling and laughing because she is a friend; rather, he is being mean and extremely unkind. "I'll show you mine if you show me yours" is an age-old edict that can become dangerous with a child who is trying to get your child to expose herself. Perhaps the child will agree to participate in the bad behavior as a way to encourage the child with special needs to act accordingly. Empowerment and recognizing the inner voice of intuition comes into play here and is discussed later, in Chapter 6.

It is important that your child learns that the one who is encouraging her to act in an inappropriate way is not really a friend. Some examples of inappropriate behavior that she may be enticed to perform are: climbing on playground equipment that is beyond her ability, stealing small items from a store, or exposing her private parts and even touching the private parts of another, or engaging in overt sex acts. These are behaviors that your child should learn are never acceptable. The doll that is encouraging the other doll to participate in these activities is not being a friend at all. The doll should immediately leave that area and tell an adult. Use the communication technique the child has to simply say "No!" when asked to participate in any such behavior.

General play

Playtime is when all children learn. They are relaxed and attending to the experience, especially if toys they enjoy are being used. Learning to say no and protecting oneself is an important lesson. When children are most relaxed, learning can be integrated and practiced without the additional stress implied in "teaching situations."

Use two dolls or puppets, preferably ones with removable clothing. One doll then forces the other to take down its underwear. The victim doll pulls up her underwear and runs away. She hides behind furniture or other toys, anything that can obscure her as she pulls up her underwear. The next day the scenario begins with the dolls playing next to each other in parallel play. This time, before the first doll has a chance to touch the underwear of the second doll, the second doll runs away and plays alone or with others. She has learned that the doll that pulled down her underwear is not to be trusted, and that it is okay to reject that doll. That doll is not a friend.

Allow your child to direct the play as much as possible. Children with an ASD may not have pretend play skills, in which case, it is important that you provide the actions for the characters. When playing, however, use as few words as possible and proceed at a slow rate so that your child has time to process the information or action you are presenting.

Even if your child does not appear to be interested in the scenes you are presenting, persist. Using a dolls house or another toy that simulates spaces that may be familiar to your child is a good starting point for some of these lessons. Play out the entire story and lesson that you are teaching at the moment. The child with an ASD may actually be paying attention, listening, and observing from afar, but not looking directly at you or the action that is taking place with the dolls.

Children with an ASD often learn in atypical ways, and as long as you present the information, you are teaching. These children may learn by visual observance and auditory input, but may not be able to attend to information or these experiences at the same time, so they may observe with use of their peripheral vision. Using more visual information and action and fewer words helps children with special needs to understand that *what* is done is much more important than the explanation or words that surround the behaviors.

For children with a cognitive delay, use one-step actions with as few characters as possible in the story. Have only one character in action at a time. Use as simple scenarios as possible; be aware of your child's level of interest and let her lead the action. Think of places and activities that are familiar to your child to use as a teaching tool.

Children with an ASD are more often able to process and understand information when that information is provided visually rather than from speech. In addition, if you know that your child will pay attention to two-dimensional information such as drawings or even the written word, use this as an additional alternative to teach your child skills.

Activities using Social Stories™

Social Stories™ are an appropriate way to reveal information for people on the autism spectrum, no matter the age. Social Stories™ were first used and developed as a method to teach children with an ASD in 1989 by Carol Gray. For Social Stories™ with one- to three-word captions, have the child color in the picture if she is unable or unwilling to draw the picture herself. Include the number of scenes in the story as you think appropriate for your child.

For example, the pictures could follow this outline:

1. Your child is playing by herself with some blocks.

2. Another child comes along to play and needs one of your child's blocks to complete his structure.

3. Your child gives or allows him to take the needed block.

4. Everyone smiles—perhaps they even build something together.

This is a simple example of sharing and being a friend.

Teaching your child that not everyone has good intentions is also important. An outline for this may look like the following:

1. Your child is playing by herself with some blocks.

2. Another child comes along and plays with some other blocks and begins to take your child's blocks without asking; soon he is taking apart the building your child was working on.

3. Your child attempts to take back some blocks and is hit by the other child.

4. Your child finds a nearby adult to intervene.

This is a difficult lesson because it is filled with nuance. It is important that your child learns to share. However, it is also important that your child does not want to be friends with someone who is harmful or who shares to the point where she is harmed. In the outline above, the harm is innocent enough— her block structure was destroyed. But what if the situation involved food? Perhaps someone is taking your child's lunch or school supplies? Children with special needs need to learn how to recognize and defend themselves against harm in all the various venues they participate in on a daily basis.

Another Social Story™ that addresses the concept of personal boundaries and private parts can look like this:

1. One stick figure or drawing of a person representing your child is sitting in the library looking at a book.

2. Another child comes along and takes your child by the hand, leading her to a place in the library that is behind a bookcase and out of view of the others in the library.

3. The second child pulls down his pants to reveal his penis.

4. Your child runs away.

Sign language as well as picture icons are popular methods that are used with children who have limited verbal skills or who are hearing impaired. If they have an augmentative communication device, it is important that a section be created for safety, as well as accurate words for all body parts, including genitalia, in the body parts section of the device. For children who have a primary level of understanding, one button can have an unhappy face icon or another picture that conveys a negative experience. Perhaps the audible voice can say, for example, "I do not feel safe!" This statement covers a variety of situations. The response of the nearby adults would hopefully be to pay attention to the child and endeavor to understand the cause of her pushing this button. The teacher or other adults should always believe that your child is feeling uncomfortable about an experience she is involved in when she expresses this feeling, and work to resolve this situation so that your child once again feels safe and happy.

Activities using role-play

For a role-play game, your child will need to have some imaginary play skills. This may be difficult for children with an ASD who generally display a concrete thinking style and have trouble putting themselves in the mind of another person. Role-play is a good way to help your child expand her empathy skills and understand the thoughts and behaviors of others.

When creating role-play, the options are endless. Use familiar locations as well as people your child knows for the happy and positive story lines. When playing out a scenario that is negative, invent another person who does not exist in your child's experience. It is important not to use someone your child knows as the "villain" of the story because you don't want your child to become confused and think that the teacher, for example, who is perfectly nice and kind, is also someone who may ask your child to touch him in an inappropriate way. Encourage your child to make up a scenario to role-play. She may use this opportunity to reveal something that has been troubling her in this safe and playful environment.

Make sure that you engage with your child at a level that is comfortable for her. Here is one scenario to act out with your child. The goal of this role-play is to teach your child how to respond if a stranger is behaving in a way that is unsafe or that makes your child feel afraid:

1. You and your child are standing in the queue at the snack bar while visiting the zoo. The line is very long and you are almost at the front.

2. Your child needs to use the toilet and cannot wait.

3. You know your child knows how to use a public toilet safely so you let her go by herself.

4. While your child is in the rest room, a stranger approaches and invites your child to see the baby monkeys (a particular favorite of your child's).

5. Your child needs to shout "No!" and return to you as quickly as possible, and tell you about the interaction.

The lesson is that under no circumstances is your child to go anyplace with a stranger.

Have your child practice loud phrases that will alert you and other responsible adults that she is in need of help. If your child uses an augmentative communication device, these phrases can be loaded onto the device as well:

- "Stop, you are not my mother (father)!"

- "Help! I don't know you!"

- "No!"

- Or, just sit down and shout—any sound at all.

How to know if someone is or is not a friend

For a typically developing child, social skills lessons are appropriate and increase skills of friendship. Children with special needs could benefit from these lessons as well, although they need an additional, if not more important, lesson—they must learn to differentiate when others are being true friends or not.

Predatory molesters/abusers act as though they are a friend to the child and may even extend that friendly behavior to others in the family. They may take their time to gain the trust of those in the inner circle of the child victim before doing anything malevolent. In addition to the physical and emotional harm being caused to the child, the child will most likely become very confused about what a friend is and how a friend should act.

In general, keeping secrets, invading boundaries, encouraging bad behavior, and making you feel bad are not experiences of friendship. Hopefully you and your child have many positive interactions and you are able to teach your child about good friendship by helping her to become aware of these people and how they are treating her. She will then have those good feelings as a comparison for when an unfortunate situation arises where someone acts as though he is her friend when the truth is that he is not.

A friend will never use coercion to convince another person to do anything. Coercion is often used by molesters/abusers to force children with special needs to act in a certain way or to perform sex acts. The child with special needs may not understand that the promise of friendship is not worth touching another person in a sexual manner or allowing another person to touch her.

What is crucial is to reinforce as often as possible that if something another person asks your child to participate in makes her have a funny feeling inside, she should say "No!" and leave the area as soon as possible. Explain to your child that while having a friend is a wonderful thing, friends do not make you feel bad.

Forming friendships during adolescence

The early teen years to young adulthood are a tumultuous time for all children. The changes that occur to their bodies, emotions, and societal expectations are vast. This is a time of great growth, but also a time of confusion and increased vulnerabilities. Now, more than ever, it is important to know who your child is spending her time with. Who are her friends?

Who are the people who are teaching and coaching her? Who are her caretakers?

Make every effort to get to know your child's friends, their parents, and how they spend their time. This is a time in life that presents a delicate balance indeed. On the one hand, we want to protect our children from all the dangers we know are in the world. On the other hand, we want our children to be as independent and self-reliant as they possibly can be. The way they act in adolescence can give us clues as to how they are reaching their fullest potential, and ways that we can guide them.

Using the internet to make friends

The internet is an invaluable tool. I have observed non-verbal children who appear to have no comprehension or awareness of the world around them go through a multi-step sequence to find the video clip they want to see or a game they want to play. But the use of the internet and competency in its use is both a blessing and a curse. While it allows all of us greater exposure to education and connections with loved ones far and near, there are also inherent dangers. At no time should your child with special needs have unlimited access to the internet.

Parental control settings are not enough to keep your child safe. Many predatory molesters/abusers find "children's" websites and pose as children. While you want to trust your child in her use of the internet, you certainly cannot trust everyone else who uses it. Keep these rules in mind and implement them to keep your child as safe as possible. While nothing is perfect, these should help limit your child's exposure to threats on the internet:

- Review the browser history on the devices your child uses, at least daily.

- Look at each website or video your child visits, at least when she visits for the first time.

- Follow all the links possible, even if you don't think your child has followed the link.

- Join your child when she is on the internet and share the experience with her.

- Under no circumstances allow your child to share photos of herself for any reason.

- If family members request photos, you should be the one to provide these.

- Do not allow your child to set up a meeting with someone she has met on the internet.

- Do not allow your child to share her daily schedule or home address with internet friends.

- If your child's school has a website, be aware and cautious about pictures they post of your child. It is great fun to see your child participating with other students during school activities, but school websites are also places where predatory molesters/abusers view and choose their victims. Make sure that the school does not provide specific demographic information about the children they post photos of.

Changing relationships: becoming boyfriends or girlfriends

As children grow and develop, they naturally experience sexual feelings. When they allow themselves to express those feelings in sexual behavior, but the other aspects of friendship stop, such as talks or leisure activities, they can be emotionally devastated. They may or may not enjoy the sexual experience. They will feel bereft when a person they thought was a true friend to enjoy all sorts of activities and experiences with becomes someone who only wants to participate in intimate activities. The child with special needs is too young to give full consent to sexual activities or feel comfortable doing so. It is important to address sexual urges and teach children to delay this behavior until they are adults and additional education can be provided.

Playing as if your child was a boyfriend or girlfriend to an older relative or teacher is not a good idea. This can become confusing because pretending about this kind of friendship is often done in a teasing way by well-meaning adults. Calling children a "boyfriend" or "girlfriend" is often met with smiles, laughs, and has a positive connotation. Children do not know that this is a tease or a joke and is not to be taken seriously. They think being called "boyfriend" or "girlfriend" is a fun, pleasant, and innocent relationship. Unfortunately, as children reach adolescence, they have not learned the true meaning of being called a "boyfriend" or "girlfriend" and the escalation of intimacy being in this sort of relationship implies. Having a "boyfriend" or "girlfriend," like having any sort of friend, is an important experience that helps the child with special needs to feel more like her typically developing friends. She may see this as growing up and having fun.

Some predatory molesters/abusers use the naïveté of children with special needs and tell them that they want them to be their "boyfriend" or "girlfriend." They then go on to tell them all sorts of sexual acting out is part of this relationship. They convince children with special needs that although they may feel funny at first, it is really okay because after all, they are "boyfriend" or "girlfriend," and this is what one does in such a relationship. This is not true. Reinforce the idea with your child that if anything does not feel right, your child has every right to say "No!" and to leave.

A true "boyfriend" or "girlfriend" will allow sexuality to unfold naturally and become mutually desired. "Boyfriends" or "girlfriends" spend a lot of time together sharing all sorts of activities that do not involve touching or sex play of any kind. If your child has a peer who is your child's "boyfriend" or "girlfriend," help them to discover mutual interests. Give them the idea that they should be doing these things as well. Do they enjoy the same kind of music? Is there a park where they like to play or a sport? Many video games have dual controls and two people compete against each other. The healthy possibilities are endless for young people with special needs to be able to enjoy each other's company.

If the individual who claims to be interested in your child in a romantic way does not have a special need, you, as the parent, have every right to question his motives. Have a frank and realistic conversation, and express your concerns. Explain that your child may not fully comprehend the nature of the relationship and that you do not want her to get hurt, either physically or emotionally.

— CHAPTER 3 —

Healthy and Expected Behavior of Family and Friends

Providing care

All children are born in a most vulnerable state. They depend on adults to keep them safe and help them thrive. Babies, generally, are able to express themselves with crying and acting fussy. These are primal responses to their needs to be fed and kept warm and dry. Children need adults to anticipate their needs to keep them safe and help them develop when they are very young. It is up to the adults to interpret the child's needs and to provide for those needs in a caring way. Child-rearing is a difficult and challenging occupation. Children who are not cared for in a healthy and nurturing way often develop sensory-processing difficulties and other disorders, although some children have delayed development even when cared for in the best possible manner.

Children born with, or who acquire, a developmental delay or any abnormality may not respond to their own needs in the same way as a typically developing peer. A child may not know she is hungry or tired, and depends on the wisdom of the adults who care for her to provide the structure and materials to maintain her health and overall wellbeing. Some children who are born with special needs have been described as very quiet and especially easy to care for, while others cannot seem to be comforted. All children are unique in how they communicate with the world and what experiences help them to feel safe and supported.

It is the right of every child to live in an environment where she can grow and learn so she may reach her fullest potential. The child born into a loving family has the innate expectation that she will be kept safe and protected. A child does not expect her adult relatives or others to hurt her or give her cause to feel ill.

Providing a safe and secure environment on a daily basis is clearly the best lesson for any child as children learn by experience and imitate the most prominent and overt behavior that they experience.

Children with special needs learn with repetition. Words are not always necessary. Repetition of safe and healthy practices becomes expected and integrated. The repetitions of experiences that are healthy provide a feeling of comfort. Even a very young child or a child with a significant intellectual disability knows when something in the daily routine is wrong.

A child integrates or internalizes feelings of nurture. She is aware of when her needs are being taking care of. This occurs at the most basic level—she knows when she is clean, comfortable, and sated. These are primal needs that need no words to understand. This understanding happens on a subconscious or physiological level. When a child is living in an environment that is chaotic and she does not know what to expect or what is happening, learning may not occur. One day this child may be bathed and fed, but another day may bring a paucity of food, harmful touching, or even sexual contact. A cascade of dysfunction occurs when the child is being molested, especially by someone she is expected to trust.

Providing a safe environment is a vital way to prevent abuse or molestation. As even the best-intentioned schools and programs are not able to keep children safe 100 percent of the time, educating your child is one of the best ways to prevent such traumatic and life-changing experiences caused by molestation or abuse.

Preventing molestation/abuse

Children with autism cover a wide spectrum of ability levels. The suggestions for activities below are general recommendations for the most common characteristics of children who have a diagnosis of autism. These include the desire for structure and routine, concrete thinking, a challenge with understanding or reading non-verbal communication, overt honesty, and difficulty understanding or empathizing with another person.

If your child is verbal, her characteristic honesty will be an asset when you are trying to understand an experience she may have had. She may not have any qualms or embarrassment when reporting an incident, and so you will be able to understand what she has experienced.

The activities below are to help your child understand expected behavioral norms of the adults and other children in her life, when she is not in her warm and loving home, or even if she is at home. These are suggestions to help teach your child about expected, safe, and healthy interactions with adults. Your child needs to learn about acceptable behavior, so that she is able to discern the differences between safe or dangerous interactions.

It is very important that your child understands that her primary or lead teacher or babysitter is a safe person. The expected safe and healthy behavioral standards are vital to her wellbeing. Teaching her appropriate and expected behavior gives her important information about when she is being treated well, and when she is experiencing something problematic.

Activities to prevent molestation: children who are non-verbal and minimally verbal

Choose a location that your child attends on a regular basis. This may be the home of a relative who is providing childcare, school, or a therapy program. Take photos of the location and use that photo as the "setting" for the play session. If your child is in the photos, this will help her to understand the play session. If photos are not an option, icons or other symbols that your child uses and understands are acceptable substitutions.

Parallel play is the most common form of play in which young children with autism engage. This play may be observed when two or more children are playing in close proximity. They may be playing with the same toys, even sharing toys from the same box or set. The children, however, will not interact with each other. Their play will be isolated in nature and they will rarely show any acknowledgement of others in the area.

1. Use dolls as surrogate children—perhaps identify one special doll or puppet as your child.

2. If possible, have pictures of the people you are representing and place them on the dolls or puppets.

3. Have the dolls peacefully playing next to each other. The dolls may be lining up cars or other toys. They may be stacking blocks or coloring on paper. The important thing to show is that the dolls are playing calmly near each other. Each doll is happy and peaceful.

4. Then say something such as, "Nice trucks" or "Pretty picture." Use minimal language, one or two words, so as not to overwhelm the child with excess auditory

information while you are using her visual learning to impart a lesson. Speak slowly and be aware that children with an ASD need time to process information. This pause has often been called the *strategic wait*. Give the child time to understand what she is witnessing. In this scenario you are acting as a safe adult who is maintaining a peaceful classroom situation for all the students.

5. Allow the dolls to participate in a common classroom conflict. Perhaps one doll bumped into the stack of blocks and they fell onto the line of trucks another doll was meticulously organizing. One of the dolls—maybe even the doll that is identified as your child—then erupts into a tantrum.

6. You immediately come over and set everything right. You prevent the situation from escalation and the dolls return to their calm play. This reinforces the message that you are the safe person (in this scenario, the teacher). You will protect the child from dangerous and out-of-control behavior. Very little language is needed in this situation. You want to teach your child that even though there are unfortunate things that happen, after the intervention of a safe adult, happy and healthy experiences (play) can resume.

Repeat a few different scenarios, even one where your child is being hit by her classmate or forced to remove her clothing. In keeping with the concept of teaching your child about boundaries, use a scenario that invades the personal body space of one of the dolls. Keep the scenes simple. This is not the time to cloud the issue with concepts of turn taking or sharing. These are, indeed, important behaviors for your child to learn, but not during this time. Depending on the attention span of your child, keep the play scenes short and simple. A good amount of time for one individual scene is three to five minutes.

Each time, the teacher will be the person who keeps everyone safe and restores order.

For another scenario:

1. Have an adult or even another child act inappropriately towards one of the dolls representing a child. Perhaps the adult will be shouting at one of the dolls or she may isolate that doll, withhold food, or not change a dirty diaper. Create a negative experience for the doll. You certainly don't want to traumatize your child, so keep the negative experience simple.

2. Have the doll that was treated poorly communicate her distress by behaving differently than usual when she returns home at the end of the day. Perhaps she refuses to eat her snack. She may be excessively quiet or throw a tantrum. Perhaps her diaper is soiled or the food in her lunch box was not eaten. Allow the doll to communicate by her actions that something untoward happened when she was away from home.

3. As the doll is behaving in this unusual way, notice and do your best to understand what has transpired. As you realize that the adult (or child) has acted badly, reprimand the person. Communicate with actions that show that you will not tolerate the mistreatment of a child and you will act to protect her. You don't want to upset your child, but teach her as gently as possible that although bad things may happen, you will not allow them to continue.

If your child shows an interest in taking over the action or corrects your manipulation of the dolls, allow her to do so. Observe the actions she has the dolls do; this is an excellent way to understand your child's thoughts and how she views the world.

Activities to prevent molestation: children with fluent speech

Some children with an ASD demonstrate a behavior that has been referred to as "hyper-verbal," that is, they may speak in complete sentences and seem to be always talking. These children may surprise the adults around them with their high level of vocabulary, but they may not always understand what they are saying—their expressive language skills will be higher than their receptive skills.

- Repeat back to the child with the preface, "What I hear you saying is…" Then, after you have summarized the statement your child made, ask for clarification along the lines of, "Is that correct?" or "Did I get that right?"

- Children who are able to read often gain more understanding from the written word than from the spoken word. Write simple sentences about what you believe your child is communicating.

- If your child is reporting troublesome behavior, listen without interruption or use questions for clarity. Allow her to get all her thoughts out. It is important to remain calm and respond quietly. Provide your child with drawing materials and ask her to draw the scenario she is describing. Believe your child. It is vital that she uses accurate words to describe body parts and behavior if she has been abused or molested. A list of alternative pronunciations has been provided at the end of this book, with a list a body parts children should know, that may not be generally taught. Also included are shortened or alternative pronunciations to accommodate children with common developmental pronunciation delays.

If your child is attending school and has functional verbal communication, the same activities as described above are appropriate, that is, you can create play scenarios that are realistic given your child's daily experiences. One difference is that you can ask the child to describe an experience when someone did not act kindly. Allow her—in fact, encourage her—to create as elaborate a scene as she likes. Have her clarify how the actors are behaving as you go along. Let her lead the scene, and pay close attention to the details she is sharing. As the play progresses, observe if your child is demonstrating any disturbing behavior. This may include touching the private parts of another, or having another adult or child touch her.

Teaching methods and tools for children with a physical disability and typical intelligence

As your child grows up, she will have different people who care for her needs. It is important that she learns to be a good director and supervisor of her care. Depending on the level of care your child requires, she may need to educate and guide a stranger to maintain her cleanliness, or perform procedures such as catheterization, diaper changes, and other quasi-medical management tasks that need to occur multiple times per day to maintain her health and overall wellbeing. It is an important life skill for your child to learn as early as possible to direct her care so she develops the ability to reach her potential.

It is important that your child knows how to care for her menstrual blood, urine, and feces, and there are myriad methods to care for these needs. You and your child and her doctor or nurse will determine the best tools and techniques for these needs. A mirror is an important tool for your child to learn how to use—you and she must not shy away from viewing her most intimate areas.

Your child should learn every step of the various procedures she needs: for example, the purpose of catheterization; the time schedule for when this should be done; the body parts to be touched and the parts that do not necessarily need to be touched; the equipment or supplies needed; and her physical position during the task (lying down on a mat, seated on the toilet, or any other position depending on her specific physical needs). She should know how her clothing needs to be managed, and how much of her body needs to be exposed.

It is also important that she be aware of the approximate amount of time each procedure should last. It is within her rights to question if the caregiver is spending an excessive amount of time with any one procedure. Caregivers who do not have the most ethical practice may use this time to delay returning to other work or as an opportunity to take a break while your child is in a stage of undress and not able to return to class. Providing your child with information about the specifics of her care empowers her to be in charge as others care for her.

Give your child the accurate language for her body parts. Instead of "hole," for example, teach the accurate word "urethra" and "labia" for girls and "foreskin" and "head of penis" and "testicles" for boys. Your child should also know the words "rectum" or "anus." Although we acknowledge that these are *private parts*, your child should understand when it is appropriate for these body parts to be touched, and the specific manner in which they should be attended to. The use of accurate terminology is important when your child communicates with another adult who is caring for her needs.

Having your child hold a mirror (if she has the functional ability to do so) is an excellent tool to make sure the adult caring for her needs is performing the tasks correctly. If your child is unable to hold the mirror so that she can see what is happening to her body, there are a variety of mirrors that can be attached to wheelchair arms or onto counters or to the thigh, or have a free-standing one. A mirror will allow your child to see what is happening to her body, especially if she does not have the tactile sensation to feel that area. It is your child's right to know what is happening to her. A mirror can also act as a deterrent of harmful conduct. In many different situations, when people know that they are being observed, or even if the possibility exists of being observed, behavior often becomes more careful and appropriate.

Young children are able to learn the proper sequence for their unique needs, and it is very empowering for your child to be able to talk an adult through a care procedure. A good idea, especially if your child attends a school with multiple aides, is for her to keep a card with the specific care sequences written out. Have this card laminated and orient your child to its location (usually in a backpack with the supplies needed). She should know how to present the card to her current caregiver. Often catheter supplies include step-by-step written directions with outlines or drawings of the body parts and the supplies necessary to properly complete the task. Laminate these directions, as they will provide the most thorough and accurate information for the procedure with the specific brand of catheter being used.

The fact that your child knows where and how an adult is supposed to touch her and, more importantly, how she is not to be touched, gives her a sense of power. If a caregiver has the impulse to molest your child, he may think twice and not touch her inappropriately. People who molest or sexually abuse children, especially children with special needs, depend on secrecy. The more your child can communicate that she is aware of how she is to be treated, the safer she will remain. Even if the experience your child has had would not be categorized as molestation, it is extremely important that the most intimate care be performed completely and correctly.

Activities to prevent molestation: children with an intellectual disability and physically typical

This category of children with special needs spans a wide array of skill and ability levels, and may be the most challenging and vulnerable population. Children may appear typical and may have developed speech so that at first glance, it may not be obvious that the child has a special need. Often children and adults who have intellectual disabilities either from birth, a brain injury, or other trauma or illness have no overt signs that they have a disability. They may not need a mobility device, or have an atypical gait or any visible scars. There is no wheelchair or other mobility device to communicate to the world that this child is different from her peers.

At times a young child will act provocatively. She may imitate behaviors she has seen in a movie or she may have witnessed a peer acting in a flirtatious manner. Often these young children do not understand that they are acting coquettishly. They may enjoy the response they garner from others of the opposite sex. At home this inappropriate behavior may appear so absurd to family members that they laugh, which only serves to encourage and reinforce the behavior. Don't fall into this trap or allow others to respond in this way. This has been used as defense by those who sexually molest young girls, claiming that the victim was encouraging of the act. There is no gray area here! It is never appropriate to touch anyone sexually without permission!

If you observe your child acting in a sexually provocative manner, address this behavior immediately. Do everything in your power as a parent to explain that this behavior is dangerous and not to be encouraged. Explain to others (adults or children) that your child simply does not understand the meaning and ramifications of her actions. The sooner you call attention to this behavior and make sure it stops, the safer your young child will remain as she grows up and moves through the world.

Do not go into details with your child about how the way she is communicating may be interpreted, as she most likely will not understand. If she is sashaying around the room, or even sitting on an adult's lap in a provocative manner, it is more than likely that she is imitating someone she has seen act this way. She does not mean to be sexually seductive. It may appear funny to see an eight- or nine-year-old or younger child sashaying around the kitchen because it is so absurd, but it is not funny. Laughing and showing approval by asking your child to repeat this behavior in a performance-like way to others will serve to reinforce the provocative actions.

Remember that children with lower intellectual abilities do not always have advanced language or communication skills. They do not understand the subtleties of a specific action as being appropriate in one setting and not in another or with specific adults and not with others, so it is important that the child stops the behavior. To prevent misinterpretation, and hopefully prevent the abuse or molestation of your child, teach your child to behave in a safe manner at all times and in all settings.

- When you observe your child acting in a provocative way, with as calm a demeanor as you can present, ask her what she is doing. Understanding what your child is attempting to communicate is what you want to know. Does she want attention from a specific person? Is she attempting to act like her favorite pop star? Does she think she is being funny? Pay attention to what your child is saying. Ask her how and/or where she learned to walk that way or say those things.

- None of these reasons for behaving in this way are generally wrong or inappropriate. Do not embarrass your child by telling her she is wrong. Instead, give her options for achieving her goals in a more appropriate manner. If your child is seeking attention from another child or adult, give her some positive ways to obtain that attention. Perhaps she can draw a picture for that person. If baking is something you enjoy doing, perhaps she can give that person a sweet gift. Children enjoy making and giving tangible gifts. A simple beaded bracelet, a drawing, or card—these are wonderful ways for children to express their love and admiration for others. The response of the recipient most likely will be positive and will reinforce this healthy activity.

- If your child is attempting to emulate a pop star or fictional character, learn about that individual who is of such great interest to your child. Perhaps the pop star likes to paint, so your child can paint like the star. Perhaps you can listen to the music together and learn the songs. If the pop star only acts provocatively or in other ways that you think are not appropriate for your child, and you do not think she is a good influence, take action. Limit your child's exposure to the pop star's music and videos. Yes, this will be a challenge, especially if your child is able to access the music and videos that you think are objectionable, but this will be a great learning opportunity and an excellent way to show your child that you are the parent and that you are keeping her safe.

- As the parent you have every right to monitor and allow or forbid your child's exposure to specific media. Many computers, televisions, and other devices have parental controls. These are good tools, but nothing is better than the words and attention of a parent. You do not need to give your child a reason other than it is your decision to not allow your child to view specific stars or shows.

- Make your wishes known in all the settings your child visits. You are the parent or primary caregiver, and you are ultimately responsible for the wellbeing of your child. One of the ways to prevent your child from engaging in behaviors she does not understand is to prevent her from learning those actions in the first place; this means that you must monitor and, yes, censor her consumption of specific information and media.

- If your child tells you that she learned these provocative movements from another child, this needs to be directly addressed. Depending on the relationship you have with the child who is coercing your child to act this way, you can approach the instigator directly. It is a good idea to get the parents of the other child involved as well. Explain to them that your child is acting in a manner that you believe is unsafe and inappropriate. Tell the child and parent that you fear for the safety of your child, that your child does not understand that the actions being imitated are harmful, inappropriate, and may lead to a dangerous situation for her. Engage the other child and parents in a conversation, explaining that your child enjoys the friendship of the other child, but that she can no longer engage in the specific behaviors with the child who is teaching your child to act this way.

Healthy activities for all children with special needs

All children should have the expectation that when they are with friends and other adults, they will learn safe and healthy behaviors. We should have the simple expectation that family and friends will honor our choice of experiences for our child.

We expect them to listen to us, and not sabotage the lessons we are teaching.

Brainstorm ways children can be friends, and find activities they can have fun experiencing together. Present some of these ideas to the other children and parents. There are many age-appropriate dance videos that children enjoy, for example. It is a good idea to show your child some enjoyable videos so that she can *teach* the other children more appropriate ways to dance—other replacement behavior could be with simple circle dances or organized dances that do not include an emphasis on pelvic movements. Enjoying safe behaviors will go a long way to preventing ongoing dangerous acting-out and extinguishing inappropriate behavior.

It would be wonderful if your child participated in Scouts or sports or any other youth group with typically developing children. This inclusive participation is worthwhile for all children, no matter the challenge or developmental disability. Children learn from their peers. Explore and find a suitable after-school activity for your child, so she has the opportunity to observe models of healthy behaviors. Scout leaders around the world must follow a code of conduct (The Scout Group 2011; scouts. ca no date). Included within that code is the rule that states that at least two adults be present to provide supervision at all times. The two leaders must be within the line of sight as well as close enough for others to hear all interactions. It is well within your rights and expectations to assure that the Scout troop your child participates in follows this code.

Addressing the issue of keeping your child safe has become a vital part of parenting, and children with intellectual disabilities need to be taught ways to keep themselves safe in all the places and situations they find themselves in.

When you think about how many different places your child is during the day and week, and all the adults she comes into contact with, it may be overwhelming, but it is your right and responsibility as a parent to know who your child is with during the day when you are not directly supervising her.

Here is a simple way to keep things straight:

1. On a calendar or a simple spreadsheet, write out the days of the week.

2. For each day, write out all the locations your child will be—don't forget to include modes of transport such as the school bus or a carpool.

3. List all the adults who are present at the various locations. If you have blank spaces and do not know who all the adults are who interact with your child, you know what work you need to do.

When your list is complete, in a calm and organized manner, ask your child about each setting and the people you have identified. (It may take a number of weeks to get through all the people and places.) If your child is so inclined you can ask her to draw a picture of the person, what he does in the classroom, or how he acts. If drawing is not an activity that your child enjoys, use dolls or other toys. Ask your child to pretend she is at Sunday school or a Scout meeting, for example. Ask her to direct the scenario. This can be very telling. Make sure to ask open-ended questions such as, "What does Mr. Tom do in class?"

Sometimes a child will convince another child to perform a sex act or commit a crime. The manipulative child may think it is funny or have the need to exert power over your child. This is a horrible form of bullying, and there are many reasons that children with special needs fall victim. It is important that your child understands the difference between a person, no matter the age, who is being a good friend and one who is not!

Give your child examples of how to behave like a good friend. Hopefully, you will be able to give many examples of when others have been good friends to your child. Some of those experiences may be when another reads a story to your child, or perhaps they enjoyed building a race track together or working on LEGO® or a puzzle. Maybe a neighbor visits and likes to play a game with your child or invites your child to go on outings. The positive experiences are endless. Some examples are simple and may be overlooked, but are important in teaching your child about "good friends" and "bad friends" (see Chapter 2).

Don't be afraid to use simple and explicit terms to get the idea across that some children or adults are just not the people your child should admire or try to befriend. Ask your child about specific interactions she is having, especially if you suspect something is happening that is not healthy or safe. As adults we often use the term "inner voice" or "little voice." We learn to pay attention to our instinct or gut reactions. Listen to your inner voice and pay attention to how your own body reacts when you come into contact with others. If you suddenly feel tense or even angry without knowing the reason, this is a red flag. Ask yourself why you are reacting this way at this time. You do not need to come to a full conclusion; just be on your guard. Your intuition is telling you something, so do your best to listen.

Children, all children, have the same feelings. They may not know how to identify these feelings, but you can help.

Activities for learning right from wrong

Depending on the level of understanding your child has about "right" or "wrong," use daily experiences to teach this lesson. Start simply. Here is one example of how the conversation may go:

1. Ask if your child knows when she is happy or sad, or if she knows if something is right or wrong.

2. Decide on a simple scenario that is repeated daily, such as a self-care task, tooth brushing, for example.

3. Help your child decide that tooth brushing is a good thing.

4. Explore the good feelings that your child may experience when she knows she is doing something healthy to take care of her teeth. This is an excellent way to help your child raise her awareness about self-care and also pay attention to how she feels about herself and her body.

5. Ask her a question that you know she will answer in the negative, such as, "Is it a good idea to brush our teeth with red paint?" Hopefully you will both share a laugh.

6. Try to get your child to explain *how* she knows this is wrong. You are helping her to pay attention to her innate sense of right or wrong. Tell her that you are proud that she has this ability; it is a very important skill. She should listen to that inner voice. Encourage her to give examples of when she listened to her inner voice. Let her know that you are very interested in what her inner voice is telling her and you want to know when she is listening.

7. Explain to your child that there are other things that are wrong and should be avoided. Some of those things are not silly like using paint instead of toothpaste.

8. Teach your child that she is an important person and is allowed to say "No!" if her inner voice is telling her that something someone else is asking her to do is not safe or she feels *funny* about it. Let her know that you will

always protect her and that no matter who the other person is who is behaving badly, you want to know.

Activities for children with multiple disabilities

Since 1974, all children in the United States have the right to a free and public education. Children with multiple disabilities are no exception to this. Throughout the day many children need to be fed, have their diapers changed, and be moved, or have their body positions altered if they are seated or lying on a mat. These are our most vulnerable children as they are dependent on others for all their needs. Prevention of harm is a priority. Children with multiple disabilities are no different than their more able peers in that they have adverse responses to negative experiences. These responses may not be as overt or easy to interpret as those of more verbal or able-bodied children, but the responses exist nonetheless.

Prevention is the best way to avoid unacceptable experiences for your child. It is important that you know and build a relationship with everyone who interacts with her. Learn the name of the lead teacher and all the assistants and paraprofessionals who may engage with your child. Review with the team on a regular basis the best methods to care for your child. It is perfectly acceptable to call a meeting to train the staff each year or more frequently, if protocols have changed. The annual Individual Education Plan (IEP) meeting is a good time to request and schedule this training session.

These recommendations are appropriate for all children, not only children with multiple disabilities. At the meeting develop a communication log, so that you know exactly how your child is spending her day. This is an expected behavior on the part of the school personnel, and you have every right as a parent to expect this request to be honored. Include in the log everything you want to know, such as (but not limited to):

- Medication administration (if relevant)

- Food and drink specifically ingested (amount eaten or ounces provided)

- Diaper changes—nature of soil

- Interactions with other students

- Educational interventions, including therapy sessions and special events such as musical experiences

- Position changes

- Child's demeanor/reactions.

Educate the team on the specific likes and dislikes of your child. If at all possible, have them demonstrate the skills they are to perform each day with your child. These may include, but are certainly not limited to:

- Feeding: Your child may be bottle-fed, spoon-fed specific textures or tube-fed.

- Diapering/dressing: Make sure you send your child to school each day with a clean diaper to start the day. Provide enough supplies for this purpose each week. Set a schedule for changing your child's diaper. Review the method for cleaning your child at each diaper change. Have a fresh set of clothing with your child at all times. Be aware of folds in clothing, labels, or other nuisances that may irritate your child's skin and cause her to be upset.

- Positioning: If your child is immobile, to prevent skin breakdown make sure your child is on a schedule to be moved and repositioned at least every two hours. Teach the staff to observe any red or irritated areas that do not resolve. Consult with your child's physical or occupational therapist to learn a variety of positions that are appropriate for your child.

When your child arrives home, observe her demeanor. If she is as happy as usual, that is wonderful. Scan your child's body for redness or any other signs of possible skin breakdown or any sign of mistreatment or molestation. After you greet your child and settle her with a favorite toy or other pastime, spend a few minutes reviewing the daily communication log. During the review, look for any unaccounted-for time periods. Also notice any new staff who may have interacted with your child during the day. When you are able to, get to know the new people who are interacting with your child. Your expectation is that everyone who interacts with your child in school does so in a loving and caring manner.

Expected behavior at home

Children need a healthy environment for growth and wellbeing. In general, everyone who enters your home is teaching your child—all children are observers. Children with an ASD have been known to remain silent in class all day, only to arrive home and repeat verbatim conversations they heard at school.

As a parent you are responsible for your child's experiences at home. Make sure your guests act in a manner that is healthy for your child to witness. If excessive alcohol or other substance use is happening in your home, make sure it is out of sight of your child, perhaps after bed time. Be aware of how the adults and older children speak and act towards each other. If you are in a difficult or even abusive relationship, seek help (some suggestions are provided at the end of this book). Demonstrating healthy and nurturing relationships helps your child to learn the proper way for adults to act towards each other as well as towards your child.

If there are periods of time that your child is out of sight and you do not know what she is doing, find out! Do not be shy about opening a bedroom door if your child is younger than ten. Respecting privacy is a good skill for your child to learn, but keeping her safe is more important. Tell your child that she is not to close the door to any room except when using the toilet, bathing, or dressing.

Monitors, cameras, and motion sensors are all good ways to monitor what is happening in your home when you are not in the same room or even when you are not at home and your child is with a babysitter. It is not necessary to keep these monitoring systems a secret. Actually, knowing that there is a monitoring system in the home is a good deterrent. If someone is thinking of acting in a malicious or deviant manner, the knowledge that there is the possibility of being observed is enough to make the person think twice before making your child a victim. Nothing, however, will replace the direct observation of a parent.

Unfortunately, abuse and molestation happen more frequently in the home setting by someone the child's parents believe to be a trusted friend or relative. The relative or friend may ask your child to sit near him or even on his lap. He may ask your child to show him her room, or if you are in someone else's home, the person may want to show her something special in another location in the house. The people in your home may give your child food to eat. Be aware of where and with whom your child is at all times.

If you notice another child or an adult acting in an unsafe manner, address the issue. Show your child that you will not tolerate hitting another person or throwing things out of frustration, for example. Tell the person who is acting poorly what kind of behavior you expect. Provide alternatives to shouting or throwing things, while still communicating the frustration that caused the outburst. When the situation is calm, review it with your child. Allow her to question the behaviors of others. Reassure her that you will always keep her safe. Let her know that if she is ever at home or anyplace else and witnesses frightening behavior, she is to tell you all about it.

Listen to her thoughts and feelings and validate them. All children have the ability to be perceptive about feelings and the emotional impact of how others act, although they do not always have the words to express what they have seen or how they feel. Without telling the child *how* to feel, tell her how you would feel in specific situations. For example, "When I see grandma and grandpa yelling at each other, I feel sad and afraid, so I leave the room."

Expected behavior in public

Everyone's behavior adjusts depending on the setting and circumstance. Home is the place where we can be most intimate and relaxed; public places in general call for more formal and restrained conduct. While singing loudly may be acceptable and even encouraged at home, this artistic expression may not be looked on favorably in the library, on the city bus, or in your favorite lunch spot. Without realizing it, we are continually teaching our children appropriate behavior. Thinking about teaching our children how others should act, especially towards them, is an important prevention tool.

In public we must teach our children to be vigilant. Of course not everyone or every place is a danger, but children with special needs, more than typically developing children, do not have discernment skills. This is an area where you teach your child in absolute—there is no gray area here.

- If someone you do not know offers your child something to eat, usually a treat, she is to say "No thank you." This may include samples handed out at a store. If your child is non-verbal, she is to sign or otherwise communicate a negative response. If there is a food that you decide is acceptable for your child to eat, have the sales person hand you the food and you can choose to have your child enjoy it or not. The child with special needs should learn that she is not to accept food from anyone unless you approve it; she is not to decide for herself.

- A child will never be in a position to *help* an adult, especially a stranger. Children may be asked to help an adult find a lost puppy or some other apparently innocent request. Of course the child not only wants to be helpful, but would also look forward to playing with a puppy once it was found. Teach your child that she is never to go anyplace with another person that you do not know, have not introduced her to, or explained to her the reason she may need to go with that adult or older child.

- Touch is a very personal and intimate act. Many children with an ASD have tactile defensiveness, that is, they are sensitive to touch and have specific feelings about the kind of touch, light or firm, and where on their body they will tolerate touch. This is an excellent defense mechanism, but not all children have it. Simply shrugging off the touch of another and moving close to you is an excellent way for your child to avoid unwanted touch. Teach your child that the touch of a stranger is not acceptable. Explain to the stranger so that your child can hear that you do not want him to touch your child. Then move away from that person.

    It is never appropriate for touching of private parts in public. As you walk through public spaces with your child, show her how people are keeping their hands to themselves. They are holding their bags or coffee cups. They may even be holding hands with each other, just as you are with your child. People are keeping their hands calm and gentle. They are not removing clothing or putting their hands down their pants or tops to touch their skin.

Teach your child that if she is ever in a situation where she feels unsafe because an adult or older child is touching her or attempting to move her away from you, she has permission to make as big a fuss as she is able. This is a time when it is acceptable for your child to throw her loudest tantrum, kick, bite, and scream. If she is verbal, teach her to say, "You are not my mommy (daddy)" or "I don't know you, STOP!" Depending on the verbal skills of your child, teach her a simple, yet loud, phrase to express her anger and fear. More than likely you will be at her side within seconds. If your child has wandered off, shouting this way will attract the attention of another well-meaning parent, police, or store clerk who will come to your child's aide.

- Using the toilet in a public setting has its own set of challenges. Not only do you want your child to learn to be independent with her toileting skills in public, you also want to maintain a certain level of hygiene. Speak in soft tones with your child in a public bathroom. Do not engage in a conversation with others. Protect your child's privacy by closing the door or curtain to the commode area and make sure her clothing is fully on before leaving the commode area for hand washing.

- A public bathroom is another setting where your child does not have the discernment skills to determine who is safe to strike up a casual conversation with and who is not. Therefore, this is another area where you and your child only speak with each other and do not engage with others.

Expected behavior in a medical setting

For most of us, the medical setting is a place of heightened anxiety. Children with special needs visit the doctor or therapist more often than their typically developing peers, so this is another setting where vigilance on the part of the parent or caregiver can go a long way to preventing abuse or molestation. Here are some guidelines to follow when your child is having treatment:

- Always have medical professionals explain exactly what they will be doing with your child.

- Be present in the treatment room if possible, and let your child see you in the room.

- There are times when a child will respond better to a therapy session or evaluation if the parent is not present. In those instances, request a room with a two-way mirror so you can view the session at all times. If a two-way mirror is not an option, request that an auditory monitor (or a baby monitor) is available so that you can listen to the session. Ask for the session to be recorded with both audio and video.

- If possible, explain to your child what she can expect from this specific visit.

- Sometimes medical examination or treatment may include the touching of private parts. You have taught your child that these parts are only to be touched by herself and by you if necessary for hygiene tasks. Now you are letting her know that it is okay for the doctor or nurse to touch them as well. Communicate that this is acceptable by being present with your child, and perhaps holding her hand during the exam or procedure.

- If something is happening that seems unusual to you, do not be afraid to speak up. Just questioning and showing the doctor that you are aware of what is an acceptable procedure on his part may cause him to resist the temptation of acting inappropriately if indeed that was on his mind.

Expected behavior in general, across many settings

These days it seems that everyone has a camera and the ability to video record anything at any time. These are wonderful tools that we keep in our pockets. We document all sorts of experiences and we can see our children grow and change with this documentation with an ease that has never before existed. For the most part, having friends, family, and even school personnel photograph your child is a positive experience. Oftentimes these photos are shared or used in albums or school yearbooks. Sometimes adults and children alike use these photos and videos for vicious and dangerous ends. Child pornography, bullying, and other inappropriate uses can result from a child being photographed. Children with special needs are especially vulnerable.

Here are some ways that you can prevent a photo or video of your child from being used to exploit or bully her:

- Ask for the written policy about photography at your child's school or day care center.

- Let the school know in writing that you do not approve of any photography of your child without your consent (written or verbal, depending on the time frame).

- Have the responsible person at your child's school inform you about how the photo will be used, who will see the photo, who will be taking the photo, and any and all information you can obtain.

- Never allow a stranger to photograph your child.

- Do not allow others to show your child photos unless you are viewing them at the same time; sometimes older children think it's amusing to show younger children or children with intellectual disabilities photos of genitals (their own or others). Children with special needs will not be able to understand what they are seeing. Any children who view pornography before they are old enough to process what they are seeing can become traumatized, even though no one has actually touched them.

- Explain to your child at her level of understanding that she is never to pose for a photo without your prior consent.

- Practice methods with your child to avoid being photographed when she does not wish to be photographed or a stranger photographs her. She can try:

  - Turning around so her back is facing the device

  - Covering her face

  - Yelling "STOP!"

  - Depressing the button on her augmentative communication device that says "STOP!" or "NO!".

It is virtually impossible to be prepared for every experience your child may have. In addition, you simply cannot expect every person your child interacts with to act in a healthy and at least neutral manner, but you can prepare your child as much as possible by teaching her that she has the right to always be treated with respect and kindness. When something untoward happens to her, it is never her fault, and she did not cause a more capable or stronger child or adult to act in a certain way. You child is certainly not responsible if the other person acts in a way that hurts her or upsets her in any way.

Different kinds of touch

We spend a great deal of time teaching our children that they are in control of their bodies, that they are the ones to determine who and how they are touched—and then we bring them to the doctor. Choose a term or picture that your child will understand for times when she is not necessarily in control of what happens to her body, so she knows that during this instance it is okay.

For medical touch, here are some delineation options that may help with this ambiguity:

- Doctor time

- Therapy time

- Cleaning bottom time

- Allowed with Mom/Dad.

If at all possible, have the medical professional explain to you in advance what will happen during a visit. Encourage the doctor or nurse to allow the child to pace the intervention. If your child needs a few seconds break, for example, after the doctor looked into her ears, encourage her to take some deep breaths and reassure her that the visit will end soon, before the doctor continues with the examination.

Communicate the anticipated experience to your child and assure her that she is to comply with the doctor's instructions. Let her know that you will be near and will try to make the experience as easy as possible. Perhaps she will be given a vaccination. Simply tell her that it will hurt her for a moment, but then she will be fine. Perhaps your child is participating in therapy and the therapist needs to support your child at the hips for stabilization. Tell your child that the therapist is holding her so that she will not fall, and she will have fun.

Explore a variety of ways your child can use her hands for touch:

- For soft touch:

  – Stroke a dog or cat and use the term "gently."

  – Feel a variety of fabric and decide which ones you enjoy (for example, velvet versus corduroy).

  – Explore the garden for new, green buds.

  – When using paints, discover with your child the difference between gently moving the brush on paper and doing so with increased pressure.

  – Lightly touch your child on her arm or head, ask her if she likes this or not, and take note of her answer.

- For firm touch:

  – Knead some dough in the kitchen or clay to make a pinch pot.

  – Scrub off some sticky food on a pan.

  – Give your child a back massage or rub some lotion or sunscreen on her arm with a firm touch, ask her if she likes this touch or not, and take note of her answer.

CHAPTER 4

Body Awareness and Life Skills

Learning opportunities

An excellent time for a child with any functional ability level to begin to learn about her body is during bathing, dressing, and other self-care activities. During bath time the child is completely undressed. This is a great opportunity to discuss boundaries and different types of touching. This is also a good time for your child to learn about her body.

While cute family names for private parts are special and help form the intimate bonds within a family, sometimes these names are not helpful. Teach your child the accurate names for various parts of the body. This is important. Private parts in general are the areas of the body that are covered while wearing underwear or a bathing suit—for boys, this includes the area covered by underpants; for girls, this includes the area covered by underpants and undershirt. The mouth is often used during molestation and should be considered a private part as well. While you do not necessarily need to teach the medical terms for each millimeter of private parts, the following names are important for your child to learn:

- Breasts
- Buttock

- Nipples

- Penis

- Testicles

- Vagina.

A list of alternative pronunciations for children who do not have full articulation or cannot pronounce certain sounds or multisyllabic words is provided in the back of this book.

Children who have not yet reached puberty should be aware of these areas of their bodies. As they grow, and begin to experience sensations and changes, it is important that this is discussed openly and clearly. Explain to your child that these areas are private. If your child does not understand the concept of privacy, simply explain that private parts are special parts of her body that she does not show to anyone. Private parts may be exposed and examined when she is in the toilet, the bath, or at the doctor's office when you are present.

Understanding the difference between public and private activities

Understanding the difference between public and private activities is also an important concept. For example, having a bowel movement is a private activity. If your child is potty-training, it is usual for a parent or teacher to be present while the child is sitting on the toilet. Your child will be learning how to clean herself and adjust her clothing during this time. Children who are independent with toilet-use learn to take care of these needs independently.

Other hygiene tasks may be done with others present, or even in public. For example, having one's hair cut or going to a salon for nail care may be a social outing, and not necessarily private. These are subtle distinctions that at times are difficult for a child with a development disability to comprehend or discern. It is important, therefore, to teach by repetition and during each experience.

The concept of boundaries

As much as possible, teach your child the concept of boundaries during real experiences. Children with an ASD or other developmental challenges do not always generalize information—for example, if a child learns that she is not to approach a stranger to request assistance in the toilet while she is in restaurant A, then the same holds true in restaurant B. Your child may need to have explicit instructions about appropriate behavior each time she is in a new setting.

Children with an ASD display an innate sense of the understanding of boundaries when they are engaged in play. They do not want another child within their immediate area to touch the toys they are using. If appropriate, use these times to explain, at your child's level, that she is asserting boundaries. Explain that her preference for being far from others and not having them touch is true for body parts and private physical functions; they are to be done alone and apart from others.

As your child develops and learns self-care skills, provide her with as much privacy as possible. Begin by handing your child the washcloth and have her wash her own body. Teach her the proper sequence from head to toe. When she washes her private parts, explain in detail how she is to clean all parts of her rectum and all the folds of the lips of her vagina. If your child is a boy, explain how to move his foreskin, if present, and make sure to clean his rectum and the underside of his testicles. Do not be shy about using real terms for body parts. If molestation occurs, you will want your child to explain clearly which parts of the body were violated, and how this was done.

Bathing protocols
Activities to reinforce the concepts of privacy and boundaries: children with an intellectual disability and physically typical

As your child becomes more competent with bathing or showering, gradually decrease the amount of her body that you wash. At first have her wash her face, then her hands. Hopefully you are teaching your child a good hand washing technique multiple times per day. The time spent on hand washing should be the same amount of time needed to sing the alphabet song or the birthday song. Follow this sequence:

1. Use one pump of liquid soap.

2. Have her scrub both her palms.

3. Have her scrub the backs of both hands.

4. Have her scrub the areas between her fingers.

5. Have her cup one hand into the other so her fingertips and her nails can rub against the opposite palm.

6. Use a nailbrush if necessary to clean excess debris from nails.

7. Rinse hands.

8. Dry hands.

In the bath tub a similar, albeit more elaborate, sequence is followed. Have your child participate in as much as possible for each part of her body. Over time she will increase her participation and you will decrease your hands-on help. This procedure can be followed in the bath tub, shower, or changing table or mat:

1. Pump soap onto a washcloth.

2. Wash face.

3. Wash arms.

4. Wash chest.

5. Wash back. (Show your child how she can hold the diagonal ends of the cloth and wash her back with one hand up near her shoulder and the other hand near her opposite hip, then reverse the hand positions.)

6. Wash legs and feet.

7. Wash genital area, from front to back.

8. Wash buttocks.

9. If your child's hair is to be shampooed, decide if this will happen first or last. If her hair is short, washing her hair prior to the rest of the body is recommended; if her hair is long, waiting until the end of the sequence is recommended so she will not be sitting with a wet head for a long time.

Daily repetition of having your child participating in the cleansing of each part of her body and naming each with one word is an excellent way to teach your child about her body. She does not need to repeat the words you state unless she is beginning to talk. As she progresses to her private parts, cover your eyes and state, "Private." Of course peek through your fingers so you can watch her in the bath tub or shower to make sure she is doing an adequate job.

When you see she is finished, ask her if she is done. Ask permission to look and complete the job as necessary. This is the beginning of her learning that certain areas of her body are for her to take care of, and even you respect this privacy.

Bathing protocol for children with an ASD with fluent speech

Begin your usual bath time routine. The sequence is the same as above. Children with an ASD thrive with consistent routines and learn best when they know what to expect. You may go so far as to state the parts of the body that are public and which parts are private. For example, you can say, "This is your arm, it is a public part. Public means that everyone can see this part."

When you clean your child's vagina or penis, you could say, "This is your penis (or vagina); it is a private part. Private means that only you and I can see this part. Keep this part covered except when you are using the toilet. Using the toilet is private; you do that alone."

By all means do not spend bath time exclusively teaching boundaries and body parts. Keep this educational conversation casual and treat it as any another conversation you may have during bath time. Bath time is a fun and often special time that you share with your child. You may be teaching your child a song and singing together. If your child is in school or a program during the day, have her review the day during bath time as well. While it is important for your child to know which parts are private, make this education a natural part of your interactions.

Giving her the vocabulary to name her body parts and the understanding to know which parts are okay for others to see and which are absolutely forbidden for others to see will provide her with a foundation of knowledge that can keep her safe.

Bathing protocol for children with a physical disability and typical intelligence

Children with limited upper or lower body strength and a range of motions or uncontrolled movements need to become the directors of their care as early as possible. Physical challenges can range from total dependence to perhaps just the need for a helping hand for balance as your child steps into the tub. No matter her ability level, the criteria she learns and understands will be the same as for all children. Use the same sequence for bathing and naming the body parts as listed above. Have your child practice this sequence and be able to direct you in her care.

Bathing protocol for children with an intellectual disability and physically typical

Follow the same sequence for bathing and naming body parts as above. Have your child repeat each part of her body and point to it as it is being washed. In addition, have her say "private" or "public" after she names each part. For example, "hair—public" and "vagina—private." This repetition reinforces the idea that different body parts are either private or public.

Bathing protocol for children with multiple disabilities who are dependent for care

The bathing sequence is the same for all children. Speak to your child and tell her what you are doing. She will feel your emotions, so please do not rush. Ask permission before progressing to each body part, and especially when you wash her genital area.

Dressing protocols

In general children learn to take off their clothing before they learn to dress. This competency begins with outerwear such as jacket and sweaters, and progresses to undergarments and those often tricky socks that need to be fitted just right at the heel and toes.

Activities for dressing that reinforce the concepts of privacy and boundaries: children with an ASD with fluent speech

When friends and relatives inquire about a gift for your child, it is a good idea to request a doll with removable clothing. Make sure the doll's clothing includes underwear. Although children with an ASD do not generally choose to play pretend with dolls, do not let this dissuade you. If your child will not handle the doll, demonstrate the dressing and undressing of the doll for your child. Make sure to use simple language and say that the doll must cover its underwear with clothing before it leaves the house. Repeat this modeling play once or twice per week.

- Pretend that another doll approaches the first doll and attempts to take her clothing off or tries to convince the doll to disrobe. The "naughty" doll may even take off her clothing or pull down her pants. Have the first doll say or otherwise communicate "No!" then run away, and seek an adult who can report the incident. For the non-verbal child, have her use her augmentative communication device or icon to express "No!" and leave the area where the naughty child is.

When your child is dressing in the morning you can follow this sequence and repeat the following:

1. Put on the bottom underwear or diaper first, then say, "Now your bottom private parts (vagina or penis and buttock) are covered."

2. Dress the top part of the body and for a girl say, "Now your breasts, your top private parts, are covered."

3. Continue dressing or helping your child dress with her remaining clothing.

4. When she is all dressed say, "You are all dressed, keep your clothes on in school."

5. Also say, "Only pull your bottoms down to use the toilet," "Do not let anyone touch or look at your private parts," and "Stay dressed."

Dressing protocol for children with a physical disability and typical intelligence

For the child who is dependent on others for her activities of daily living such as bathing and dressing, putting her in charge of these procedures helps her to become a strong advocate for her own care and safety.

Teach your child that her bottom underwear is to be put on first. While this may not be convenient for caregivers who may want to dress a child from top to bottom to decrease the amount of lifting or maneuvering they need to do, this is not acceptable as it will prolong the amount of time your child's private parts are exposed. Teach your child to be assertive as she has every right to be cared for in the best and most dignified manner possible. Teach her to direct her own care. Have her state that this sequence is to be followed. If necessary, have the sequence written out on a laminated card for the caregivers so there is no confusion as to how your child's specific care is to be provided. Here is an example:

Dress or help (name of child) in the following sequence:

1. Bottom underwear or diaper

2. Bra or undershirt

3. Pants

4. Top or dress

5. Socks

6. Shoes

7. Sweater or outerwear.

Maintaining a consistent routine as well as reinforcing the concept of privacy helps to establish your child's belief in herself and others that she deserves dignity and privacy, no matter her physical abilities.

When a physically challenged child experiences a consistent routine, she will know what to expect in terms of her care. She will learn to expect specific sensations and depending on her skill level, will move her body and assist with her care in an ever-increasing way. This increased level of function is only possible if your child has consistent repetition of the motor interventions and has the opportunity to assist over time.

Dressing protocol for children with an intellectual disability and physically typical

Children with intellectual challenges can learn to be aware of the parts of the body and to protect themselves from inappropriate touching. Repetition of the above dressing sequence should be reinforced when teaching dressing skills. At times parents are in a rush and decide that it is easier for them to perform a self-care task for the child than to wait for the child to do the task independently. It is important not to give in to the desire to rush the task along.

Taking away the opportunity for your child to complete the self-care task of dressing because it is taking too long is doing a great disservice to your child. The goal here is for your child to be as independent as possible. If you are in the habit of performing tasks for your child because you can do it quicker and better, you are teaching your child that she is not a capable person. The lesson, instead of one of competence and self-reliance, becomes a lesson of learned helplessness. The parent who does most things for the child sets the child up for being in the control of others. This child is not learning to be aware of her own body and is accustomed to being moved and manipulated by others. This may set her up for not having the awareness of when a touch is inappropriate and which parts of her body are private or public.

The following suggestions are important for the parents and caregivers of children who are physically competent to incorporate into interactions with these children so they learn a foundation to maintain their own safety:

- Allow more time than your think necessary for daily dressing.

- Use one-step directions, that is:

  1. Put one leg into the leg opening of your underwear.

  2. Then put the other leg into the leg opening of your underwear.

  3. Then pull the underwear up so it covers your bottom and vagina/penis.

- Provide one piece of information at a time, such as "Your underwear covers private parts" and "No one touches your private parts."

- Breathe deeply and do not rush.

- Repeat the same dressing sequence daily:

  1. Bottom underwear or diaper

  2. Bra or undershirt

  3. Pants

  4. Top or dress

  5. Socks

  6. Shoes

  7. Sweater or outerwear.

Give your child as much time as she needs and don't rush to correct her effort if she gets it wrong. Give her time to self-correct—a great deal of learning is done by trial and error. Allow for a less than perfect appearance. It is more important for your child to learn the names of her body parts, which parts are private, and which are public than it is for her to appear perfect. After she is dressed, simply state, "Clothing stays on in school. No one touches your clothing or tells you to take off your clothes at school." The repetition of the instruction that she is not, and nor is anyone else, to remove her clothing, will help her to learn this lesson.

Dressing protocol for children with multiple disabilities who are dependent for care

Use the same mindset for dressing as you do during bathing your child, with dignity in mind. Speak slowly and calmly to your child. Help her into her clothing in the same sequence each day. You may be surprised by how much help your child is able to contribute to the dressing process when she is allowed to learn the procedure through daily repetition. Use the same sequences provided above.

Grooming protocols

Grooming refers to any task that refines an individual's appearance. Grooming tasks are usually done by children who have fair to good fine motor skills. Just as with any other skill, children with different functional levels are able to participate in these skills at times with modifications or adaptive equipment. Grooming tasks include tooth care (brushing and flossing), nail care, hair brushing and styling, sunscreen application, and makeup use.

Some children have an interest in appearing older than their years, which may be accomplished with the use of makeup. Indeed, there are many makeup products on the market specifically for children who are younger than teens. Appearance is a public form of communication—the clothing and grooming styles, specifically the amount and style of makeup worn, tells the world how the person views herself and how she wants others to see her. If a young child wears makeup that allows her to look older than her years, she is communicating, intentionally or not, that she believes she is older than her age. It is not too far a leap for others to then believe that the child is capable of acting older than her young age.

Be very aware if and when your child begins to show an interest in makeup, and objectively observe how she looks and how others may interpret that appearance. Sadly, as a defense of their criminal actions, some molesters state that the young girl "asked for it" and point to a manner of dress and how the child comported herself. Of course any kind of appearance is not an excuse for a child to be molested at any time. However, you do not want your child to increase her chances of being a victim due to a specific behavior and the use of makeup when her intention was to look pretty and not provocative.

Participation in grooming is often relaxing, although when someone is relaxed, self-awareness and protective responses may lessen. Some molesters may use the offer of brushing hair or doing a manicure or pedicure as an opportunity to have the child become accustomed to the touch of this person. Be aware of who is touching your child at all times. If someone offers to provide or perform grooming for your child, pause, and think about it. Ask yourself the following questions:

- What is my and my child's relationship with this person?

- Is this offer random or appropriate for the situation?

- Have I mentioned that my child needs a haircut or wants to have her hair braided, for example?

- How does the person offering respond when I say that I would like to participate in the grooming activity as well?

Listen to your own intuition. You do not need more of a reason to decline the offer of grooming for your child other than you are the parent and would rather not accept the offer.

Toilet-use protocols

Protocols are simple one-step consistent directions that help children learn to perform daily activities consistently and correctly. It is a good idea to follow each sequence in the same manner each time the task is completed. When the same routine is adhered to on a daily basis, the activity becomes rote and children are able to increase their level of competency.

Toilet-use protocol for children with ASD and children with an intellectual disability and physically typical

Children with an ASD are usually visual learners, that is, they are able to process and use the information presented to them if it is offered visually more often than if it is given with words. Physically demonstrate as much of the applicable actual procedure as possible for the child. When she is able to witness a task, she has the opportunity to learn in a way that is easiest for her. If at all possible, allow the same-gender parent to use the bathroom as the child observes. Use simple one- or two-word phrases to describe what you are doing and how you are taking care of yourself. For example, an interaction may be something like this:

1. Close the door.

2. I'm taking down my pants and underwear.

3. I'm making pee.

4. Now I clean my body's buttock, or penis/vagina, using only my own hand.

5. Now I pull up my clothes.

6. Now I flush.

7. Now I wash my hands.

8. Now I can open the door.

Have the child use the toilet during the same period of time. Make sure to especially reinforce the idea of closing the door completely and only using her own hands to manage her clothing and clean her body. Over time, decrease the amount of actual hands-on assistance that you provide. If this is the time of life when your child is being toilet trained, this is a good time to read her favorite book about toilet training.

Use photos of the child engaging in each activity. Have the child place these in the sequence of activities prior to using the bathroom. Another teaching option is to use the photos or icons as a picture exchange system. Reinforce the concept that only the child is to touch herself while in the toilet, and no one else. The exception here is if the child is not yet independent; only then it is appropriate for another to clean her and assist with clothing management.

Toilet-use protocol for children with fluent speech

It is not unusual for children with fluent language skills to have a higher expressive level than receptive—that is, they may not always understand the words they are saying. It is a good idea to show pictures to this child as well. You can say, "Here's a reminder of what we do in the toilet" as you hand her a book. Make sure to tell the child that the door needs to be closed when she is using the toilet.

Public toilets have a variety of logistical situations that require some navigation. Some have a single commode and sink in one room while others accommodate multiple people with individual stalls and a communal sink area. Different toilets have different door-locking mechanisms.

- Each location that your child visits for the first time warrants a visit with you. Have her demonstrate to you that she is capable of closing and locking the door from the inside.

- Wait outside the door. When she is finished, make sure she is able to open the door again when she has used the bathroom, washed her hands, and is completely dressed. Impress upon your child that she is to be completely dressed before she opens the door.

- If she requires assistance with a button or zipper, have her pull up her bottoms and secure them to the best of her ability. Wait outside the door as she opens it, so that you can obscure her view from anyone else in the area while you assist with the final steps of dressing.

- It is a good idea for you to use the toilet first, while she waits outside. If you do not think she will stay right outside the door, then by all means have her in the stall with you. This is a way that you can familiarize yourself with the specific lock and problem-solve any idiosyncratic issues that may arise.

As your child reaches the developmental stage when she is independent in the toilet, repeat the "rule" that only she is the one who touches her "private parts." Take advantage of the characteristic of most children with ASD and be very concrete about this. It is a "zero tolerance" area.

Toilet-use protocol for children with a physical disability and typical intelligence

Bowel and bladder care is perhaps the most intimate and sensitive part of the child's day. If she was born with a disability that necessitates the need for her to be totally cared for in this manner, she has become accustomed to others touching her to empty collection bags or to catheterize her. If she has become dependent recently due to an injury or illness, she may need some time to become used to others caring for her in this way. No matter how long it has been that your child has required toileting care, give her as much control of this function as possible:

- Make sure she is aware that her caregiver needs to follow proper hygiene procedures, which include, but are not limited to, good hand washing and the use of disposable gloves.

- Have her know the specific supplies needed to care for her specific needs.

- Have her keep an inventory of needed supplies in a specific location; this may be her backpack or a cabinet at school or in the bathroom she uses.

- As she gets older, have her responsible for informing you when her supply is running low and the need to replace those supplies. Some supplies may include:

  – Disposable gloves

  – Cleansing wipes

  – Diapers

  – Catheters

  – Specific ointments or medications

  – Any other tools or supplies unique to her care.

- Make your child responsible for the time schedule or frequency of her bowel and bladder care, that is, have her inform the person caring for her when the time for care arises and what supplies are needed.

- Have her know and be able to verbalize each step in her care.

- Have your child know approximately the amount of time each care procedure should take.

• As described in the previous chapter, a mirror could be made available so your child is able to monitor and assess the accuracy of her care.

Toilet-use protocol for children with multiple disabilities

There is a wide spectrum of children who can be in this category. For children who are non-verbal as well as physically dependent, it is important that you know who is caring for your child when you are not present. Make sure that you train these caregivers in the proper procedure necessary to keep your child clean and healthy. Have the caregivers demonstrate proper technique, hygiene adherence, and supply-use.

After your child returns home from school or her day program, check to make sure she has been cleaned and appropriately attended to during the day. It should be fairly obvious if the diaper, for example, has been on for an extended period of time. If it is saturated with urine or feces, it has been on for too long.

Provide the school with a specific time interval schedule for changing and cleaning your child. Make it a point to educate all class staff about the proper protocol for the toileting needs of your child. Reinforce this education with the adjunct staff or anyone who may have responsibility for caring for your child.

Adolescence

The onset of adolescence is a one of the most intense growth spurts your child will experience. Changes take place physically, emotionally, and in the way she is seen by others. This is an especially challenging time for the child as well as her parents. Just about every aspect of life will change for the child during this time, which can last for a year or two.

Exploring sexuality

Sexuality is a normal, healthy, and beautiful part of life. Sexual feelings and exploration are a normal and natural part of growing up. Adolescents and young adults develop the same feelings and urges as their typically developing peers. Speaking frankly with your child about these feelings and behaviors can help her to remain safe, while at the same time enabling her to enjoy life.

Make every effort to put aside your own embarrassment and hesitancy about this most intimate subject and discuss this issue with your child at the first signs that she may be showing an interest in sexual behavior.

Masturbation

Physical sensations in the genital area will develop. Let your child know that this, too, is an important part of her natural body growth and nothing to feel alarmed about. Masturbation is a natural way to relieve sexual tension. Many children with special needs discover this independently. Bringing up the subject of masturbation without shame or judgment allows your child to feel safe. If she has been participating in masturbation and is worrying about it, she will feel relieved after the conversation. If she has not been masturbating, bringing up the subject will not cause her to engage in this behavior until she is ready, if at all.

Tell your child that although masturbation is not a bad thing to do, it is a private activity, and privacy rules apply:

- Masturbation is something that is done alone.

- She is free to masturbate in the privacy of her own room.

- She is not to talk about masturbation with others.

- She is not to show others how she does it.

- If she gets the urge to masturbate while at school or another public place, she is to wait until she is in a private space at home.

Review with your child the concepts of boundaries, privacy, and saying "No!" as well as the concepts of friendship that we have discussed. Allow your child to express her feelings and opinions about sexuality. Assure your child that these new and confusing feelings are normal. Let her know that she does not have to participate in any sexual behavior until she is in the right relationship, and at the right time, and if she chooses to participate. If you have religious guidelines that specifically address this issue, this is the time to teach those rules, if you have not already done so.

Physical changes

Your child may notice increased hair growth under the arms, on the legs, and the face, as well as an increase in the size of genitals and breasts. Your child will perspire more and produce body odor. You will notice these changes as well. This is a good time to add deodorant to the bathing and dressing sequences you have already been perfecting.

For girls reaching puberty, this means the onset of menses. Provide products for your child that you are confident she can manage, that is, have her use pads instead of tampons at first. Answer any and all questions for her. Specifically delineate a time schedule for her to change her pad to avoid any embarrassing odor or leakage. Telling a child with special needs that she should change her pad "as needed" is not specific. Tell her to change her pad each time she uses the toilet.

Assure your child that the changes she notices are normal and a natural part of becoming an adult. She may be very interested in these changes and have a lot of questions. Answer the questions at the level she asks. Only respond to the questions she asks without adding additional information or going off on a tangent.

Make every effort to be objective and calm with your answers. If you are embarrassed or squeamish about these changes, your child will notice your discomfort. She may conclude that something is awry with the changes that are happening to her body. This may prevent her from asking you for clarification in the future. You want your child to come to you with questions and not to other people, so take a deep breath and know that answering her questions is important.

Emotions

As children become adults and go through puberty, hormones are released. These not only facilitate physical changes, but emotional ones as well. They may cause your child to be hungry or tired or have extreme mood swings. This is an extreme growth spurt time and requires a great deal of patience for parents to navigate through.

Help your child to understand that she may at times feel agitated or sad and not understand the reason for this. Encourage her to speak to you when she is having strong feelings, and assure her that you are available for her to share her thoughts. Let her know that we all have many feelings, and this is also part of growing up.

Communication

Make sure your contact information is listed in the section "ICE" (in case of emergency) on your child's phone. Make sure to review her calls, texts, and her other uses on a daily basis. Having a cell phone is a great tool for communication and safety. Unfortunately, however, a cell phone can also be used for bullying or for a pedophile to contact and manipulate your child. Reviewing how the phone is being used frequently is one way to increase your awareness of your child's experience when you are not with her. Daily review is not excessive and is a good way to let your child know that you are interested in her life.

Review privacy concepts, and make it a rule that your child NEVER sends a photo of herself without clothing on to anyone at all. If she wants to send her friend a photo of a new outfit, for example, have her show you the photo first, and with your permission, send it.

When your child first gets her phone, begin the habit of reviewing its use with her daily. This way she will not think it is out of the ordinary or an invasion of her privacy. If she is not an adult, or a totally independent adult, you have every right to know who she is communicating with. This is a good way to help her to stay safe.

Tell your child not to provide her phone number to anyone without your permission. This will prevent her from receiving text messages or photos from strangers.

There are apps designed specifically for children that reinforce safety. These help children contact approved people if they are in need of help of any kind (see some suggestions at the end of this book).

Tell your child that she is not to give out her home address to any new friends. If they want to come and visit, you will make the arrangements.

It is important for your child to know how to contact you if she needs help or in case of emergency.

Independent travel on public transportation

If you are fortunate enough to live in a city with public transportation, learning to use the bus or rail system is an important life skill for your child. Teach her the following rules about using public transportation independently:

- Have the pass or money in your hand before approaching the bus stop or train station.

- Follow the cue to board with the other passengers.

- Do not speak with strangers.

- Do not stare at other passengers.

- Do not tell a stranger where you are going or what you will do once you arrive.

- If a stranger asks if he may join you when you get to your stop, the answer is "No!"

- If a stranger is sitting too close and you feel uncomfortable, move your seat or standing place.

- If you feel scared or bothered in any way, tell the driver or conductor.

- Do not accept help with books or packages when you get off the ride, even if you are struggling with your belongings.

- Always wear shoes that are comfortable so you are able to walk quickly or run if needed.

As your child is learning to use public transportation, have her practice with you as many times as it takes for you to feel confident that she can be independent. Use public transportation with her during all the different times and days that she potentially may be using it. The characteristics of the people who are passengers as well as the schedules the vehicles run vary according to the number of riders at specific times of the day.

CHAPTER 5

Who to Tell and How to Tell

Steps to Take

First steps

If you suspect that your child has been molested or abused, the first thing to do is take a deep breath. If, in fact, molestation has occurred, the last thing your child needs is to see you out of control with worry and upset. This control of your own emotions and impulses is, of course, very difficult, but necessary. If your child is non-verbal or does not have the ability to verbally report the molestation, the steps to take are the same as if your child has provided a detailed verbal account.

You, as the parent or primary caregiver, may not be the one who discovers or suspects the molestation of your child. If your child attends school or a residential or day program, the people employed by those institutions are mandatory reporters—employees or volunteers who, by virtue of the nature of their position, are legally bound to notify legal authorities if abuse, neglect, or molestation is suspected.

The list of people who are obligated to report suspected mistreatment of a child is very long and the specific laws are different depending on local laws. In general, anyone who comes into contact with a child is a mandatory reporter. This includes staff and volunteers at schools, childcare centers, churches, sports clubs, therapists, and so on.

Once you suspect that your child has been molested:

- Do your best to remain calm.

- Assure your child that you believe everything she has reported to you.

- Help your child to understand that she is not at fault and the other person is the one who acted badly.

- Let your child know that you will keep her safe and not allow harm of any kind to continue.

- Allow your child to communicate as much or as little as she wants to when this issue first arises.

- Do not press your child for details.

- Contact the nearest child advocacy center—these are specifically designed to help your child during this time. (A resource list of centers is located at the back of this book.)

- Contact law enforcement.

Getting help

Once you have made the initial contact with a child advocacy center, and have arranged a time for a visit, bring your child to the center for help. Most molestation reporting does not occur immediately after the child has been molested—it is not uncommon for molestation to be happening over a period of time.

No matter when the molestation is reported in relation to when it occurred, your child will receive care and the perpetrator will be dealt with by the legal authorities in your area.

Every state within the United States and every country in Europe has individual statutes of limitations, that is, each location has individual laws that determine the amount of time after the illegal act has taken place that legal charges may be brought. Do not think about the time frame. When you discover the molestation has happened, report the crime and seek help. It is never too late to show your child that you will take care of her. Taking steps to report this crime and helping your child through the process of healing takes great courage and is an expression of the deep love you feel for your child.

After contacting the advocacy center nearest to you, set an appointment as soon as possible. Once you and your child arrive at the center, you will be assigned an advocate. Advocacy centers are designed to be warm and welcoming for the child. The experts who work there know how difficult this time is for your family and they do everything they can to make sure the harm ends and the healing begins.

The first visit to the advocacy center

Advocacy centers are usually filled with books, stuffed toys, blocks, and soft furniture. The environment is designed to encourage the child to feel as relaxed as possible so she can tell the story—if she is able—about the experience of the molestation.

Children are not given a snack before the initial interview, as the center does not want to appear as though they have been bribing the child in any way to tell a specific story. Make sure that you bring along your child's augmentative communication device if she uses one. If your child has a special toy or item that provides comfort, allow her to have this item as well when you visit the advocacy center. The initial visit may last many hours and may proceed in this way:

- If your child does not wish for her parent or any other caregiver to be present during her visit at the center, this wish must be honored. There are waiting rooms available which are made to be as comfortable as possible. Remain at the center—your child may change her mind and decide she does actually want you with her during all or part of the process at the center.

- With the parent and advocate present, a social worker or other professional who is expert in working with children will interview your child. This is called the forensic interview.

- Your child will be asked open-ended questions and given as much time as she needs to tell about her experience; this may take more than one session.

The examination

A physical examination will be done—often there is no physical damage to the genitals, but this does not mean that sexual molestation has not occurred. The child may request you be present or not, and this needs to be the child's choice. The physical examination will include:

- A complete physical, so as not to focus solely on the genital area. It is important to have a complete picture of the child's overall health as well as any signs of abuse or trauma on all areas of the body, and not just the genital area.

- Your child will likely be requested to assume a number of positions including on her back, on her side, and on her back with her knees bent up to her chest. If she is unable to move independently, the medical practitioner will help her into these positions.

- The doctor or nurse may spread the labia gently with fingers in sterile gloves. No insertion into the vagina will occur during this examination—this is not the pelvic examination women receive during a gynecological examination and is not as invasive. An internal pelvic examination will NOT be performed.

- A colposcopy examination may be done. This is an instrument that does not touch the child's body, but it does provide light and magnification of the genital area. Photography is also an option with the use of this tool, which can serve as evidence of damage or irritation of the genital area. Other technology may also be used as part of the examination.

- Dry cotton swabs may be used to collect samples if the doctor suspects that this may be helpful in determining the presence of disease or any DNA of the perpetrator.

- Your child may stop the examination at any time or refuse any part of the examination.

- The professionals present will honor the wishes of your child, and proceed at the rate she prefers.

- It is important that you do not ask the professionals questions or interrupt the process during the examination, and allow the trained experts to interact with your child.

- Your role during the examination is to assure your child that she is now safe and to provide comfort as needed.

Special considerations and methods to consider during the examination for children with an ASD

Children with an ASD, no matter their verbal ability, understand communication if it is presented visually. Doctors and nurses are wonderful at explaining the process of a physical examination, and may even have models that they can use to show your child exactly how they will perform the examination and which, if any, instruments will be used. The following suggestions will be useful to present to the healthcare provider prior to the start of the physical examination:

- Request that the healthcare provider who will be performing the examination shows your child how they will examine her and how they will touch her using the model, with only one or two words as an explanation of each step.

- Request that the healthcare provider uses the *strategic wait* method for communication, that is, request that the provider gives one instruction or bit of information at a time and waits for up to 30 seconds for the child to process the information. Allow for silence.

- If your child uses an augmentative communication device, allow her to have the device and to use it during the examination to ask questions or communicate the wish for the exam to be paused at any time.

- Have a physical item or token to represent each step of the process. This will provide your child with visual information that shows her how many steps the examination will take and how she is progressing through the process. For example, if using a paper chain with ten rings, have your child tear a ring for each step of the process, if she is capable; tear off one ring as a step is completed. You or the healthcare provider can also perform this task.

- Have a preferred activity ready for your child to engage in after the examination. This may be a favorite snack or book or toy train. Using the *first/then* process during the examination will help your child think of the future and help her to look forward to something she enjoys.

Special considerations and methods to consider during the examination for children with a hearing loss

No matter what method your child uses to communicate, make sure to have it available during the examination. If your child has a person who interprets using sign language, have a familiar interpreter, if at all possible. Have the interpreter positioned so that your child has a view of the interpretation while at the same time having her privacy protected during the exam. The medical professional can accomplish this with the use of sheets and requesting that the interpreter move to various locations in the room during different parts of the examination.

Special considerations and methods to consider during the examination for children with physical challenges

Children with multiple physical challenges may not be able to assume or maintain the various positions required during the physical forensic examination. As the parent, you know how your child moves and if she is able to maintain her body in specific ways. If your child uses various positioning devices such as pillows or wedges, bring these items to the center for use during the examination. If your child is able to be in the physical positions requested by the healthcare provider, she will be able to have as complete an exam as possible.

After the examination

Once the examination is completed, allow your child time to regain her equilibrium. If she has a favorite toy or other comfort item, allow her to keep it with her during the entire process. Do not question your child or encourage her to talk or otherwise communicate about her experience. Allow your child to speak and share her experience with you at her own rate.

Emphasize that you do not think your child did anything wrong and that you are not angry or upset with her. While it is important not to minimize the extent of harm that has been done to your child, it is also important that this experience does not define her or your family.

Be close to your child and return to your usual routine. If the initial visit ends late in the day, most likely the afternoon and evening routines have been disrupted. Getting back on track as soon as possible will help to decrease the trauma and disruption that has already occurred.

Keep these ideas in mind:

- Eliminate any contact your child may be scheduled to have with the suspected perpetrator. If the perpetrator is a close family member or friend and resides in the home with the child, this may be a great challenge to arrange, in which case, you may want to:

  - Contact a trusted friend or relative and request an impromptu evening or even sleepover at her home. Provide your friend with as much or as little information as you feel comfortable sharing. If you tell your friend that you do not want to go into details at the moment, a good friend will honor your request and help you and your child without question.

- Using as much assertiveness as you are able, simply tell the perpetrator that you and your child will not be at home (or visiting) and that you will contact him later.

- Focus on your child and her specific needs at the time—this is not the time to confront the perpetrator.

- Have your friend or relative retrieve needed items from your home. Give your helper a specific list of what will help your child feel comfortable and safe. This may include pajamas, clothing, toothbrush, and a favorite bedtime book. Don't forget to ask for clothing for yourself and for your child for the following day.

- Let your friend or relative know that she does not need to engage in conversation or explain anything to him if the suspected perpetrator is in the home while your friend is retrieving the items for you. Have her simply state, "I am getting these things for my friends." She does not need to provide any information, including your location.

• Return to the usual routine your child follows as soon as possible. Do not augment the harm already caused by the molestation by disrupting your child's school or recreational activities.

• Get help for yourself so that you can process this experience.

- When your child is calm and perhaps asleep, contact any other family members or friends who you believe may be in imminent danger from the suspected perpetrator.

Legal action

Law enforcement needs to be notified of any suspicion of such a crime against a child. You do not need to have absolute evidence that the molestation has occurred; suspicion is adequate to prompt an investigation.

In many cases the advocacy center will share the information provided by you and your child with the police or local legal authority. Staff employed by advocacy centers are mandated reporters, so this reporting does not violate any confidentiality rules. The police will work closely with the medical and other professionals to treat your child with as much sensitivity as possible. Many jurisdictions have specially trained teams that respond to these specific kinds of crimes (see, for example, Voices Carry Child Advocacy Center no date).

Protective custody

In some cases, due to the overarching priority of keeping your child safe, she will be taken into protective custody and placed in a safe location. The criteria for removing a child from home vary depending on where the child lives. In some cases, any suspicion of sexual molestation will instigate immediate removal from the home until a full investigation is done. If the investigation finds that the child can safely be returned to her home, she will return. Some jurisdictions require a judge's order to remove the child from the home.

As more legal procedures are being completed via the internet, the procedure for obtaining a warrant to remove a child has become quicker.

If the child is removed from the home, she will not be returned home until the authorities are confident that the child will be returning to a place and responsible adults who will keep her safe from harm. Law enforcement is aware that removing the child from her home further compounds the trauma she has already experienced, and this is only done as a last option. Law enforcement personnel also realize that working with the social worker and other professionals on the team is vital in protecting children and bringing the perpetrator to justice.

Family

Statistics reveal that most abuse and molestation of children is perpetrated by a close family member or friend. The molestation may have been happening for years until it is brought to light. Signs may have been ignored about the inappropriate behaviors and interactions by someone who is an important part of the family, by someone who is loved by all.

In other cases, the perpetrator may be someone who is feared by others in the family in addition to your child. It may be an adult who has strict rules about how the home and family are to be organized and run. It could be that this person is someone who has been violent with family members. If he has not been physically violent, then maybe he controls others with emotional abuse. It is easy to underestimate the control one person may have over another without ever using violence.

Dependency on the abuser

Some people who believe that they are totally dependent on another for the necessities of life may tolerate all kinds of abuse if they believe their support and the wellbeing of their children are dependent on another person. They may sacrifice their own happiness if they believe they are being taken care of. This is a dependency trap that some women may fall in to. A woman who does not have her own means of financial earning is vulnerable to this situation. If this woman has a child with special needs, she may be willing to overlook an authoritarian partner or even being abused herself for the support of her child.

Finding help and strength

If a woman finds herself in these circumstances it is important to seek help. Many communities have shelters and support services for women and women with children who need to leave abusive situations and who have no other place to turn.

Even if the mother has a job and the skill to support herself and her children without the need of another income, she may still feel powerless. The cultural pressure to keep the family together or to take responsibility for anything that happens in the family may cause the mother to feel powerless to change the abusive circumstances. If a woman finds that she is in this kind of situation, it is important for the wellbeing of her children to get out. Perhaps a trusted friend can help her to find the social service agencies that can support her through the transition and help her to gain some much needed inner strength so she can best provide a safe home for her children. It is possible to learn a skill and raise children in a safe, secure, and healthy home without depending on an abusive person who is harming a child.

The fact that the person harming the child is someone she loves and who seems to be loved and respected by other members of her family is extremely difficult for a child to reconcile, especially a child with a developmental disability. The child most likely has warm feelings for the individual who is hurting her and violating her trust at the same time. How, you may ask, is this possible? Parents may also have conflicting feelings towards the perpetrator.

Possible reactions of other family members, and your own response

Some families are torn apart. At times the victim and her family become the target for anger because the abuse has been brought to light and "torn the family apart." Other family members may have suspected that molestation has occurred and are complicit in keeping the secret, and may feel guilty about enabling the molestation to continue. Stay strong and keep your child and her safety as your first priority. No one and nothing is more important that the healing of your child and her feeling safe again so that she is able to reach her full potential. Your child has every right to be heard, believed, and allowed to grow and flourish.

Some families simply refuse to believe the child and the parent(s) who are seeking help for their child. They may discount the reports of the child, pointing out the fact of the disability, and coming to the conclusion that anything the child says has no validity. They may point out instances when the child lied or told an unreliable story. They may say the child does not have the ability to discern right from wrong. As difficult as it may be to hear all of this, stay strong. Simply let them know that the fact is you believe your child and you are seeking help for your child and for yourself. You are also pursuing legal action against the perpetrator. It is important that you let your family and friends know that you need their support at this time. If they choose not to believe you or attempt to dissuade you, let them know that you are going to continue on this path because you believe it is the best course of action for your child.

Do not waste your time or energy attempting to convince other people who do not want to be convinced. Just let them know that they are entitled to their thoughts and opinions, as are you. This is a sad and difficult situation, so please seek support and help for yourself as well as for your child. It may help to keep in mind that your child comes first, and sad as it may be, you need to choose your child's wellbeing and safety over all others.

Family gatherings

If the perpetrator is a member of the family, then family gatherings will change. Depending on the responses of the other members of the family, holidays and other gatherings may be more or less joyful. There are probably as many different reactions to the fact of the abuse/molestation and the experiences that followed when the information is brought to light as there are members of the family. Take a deep breath and stay strong in the knowledge that you are being an excellent parent.

Moving on with life

Changing school, church, sports club, or any other community setting where the abuse or molestation occurred may be a good idea. If you have learned about a specific molester and have reported him, he should be immediately removed from contact with children pending due process. If he is allowed to continue, then remove your child from the program. Find an alternative or replacement activity for your child.

If you do succeed in having the perpetrator removed from the organization where the molestation occurred, you are doing a great service. It is likely that he is molesting other children or may have plans for other victims in the future. You will probably help more children than you realize when you help your own child.

— CHAPTER 6 —

Personal Empowerment
Feeling Strong and Safe

Listening

As Henry David Thoreau[1] said, "The greatest compliment that was ever paid me was when one asked me what I thought, and attended to my answer." The act of listening happens with more than just the ears. Listening is a whole body experience. When we really use our body, our eyes, and our mind in specific ways, more communication happens without words, with non-verbal communication.

The following suggestions are appropriate for use with children with all functional levels.

Non-verbal communication of the listener

- Face the child you are listening to.

- Turn your body in the direction of the child.

---

1   Thoreau was an American philosopher who lived in the Northeast of the United States from 1817–1862. He is well known for his iconic book *Walden* which was published in 1854.

- Look into the child's face or at the device or picture icons she may be showing or pointing to. Return to face the child.

- Put down your smartphone, newspaper, or anything else you might have been engaged in before your child initiated communication.

- Keep your hands calm and still.

- Do not interrupt or ask questions before your child has finished telling you what she needs to say.

- Attend to the words or other verbal communication.

- Observe your child's body language as she communicates:

   - Is her speech rushed or pressured?

   - Is the vocabulary being used at her usual level or a decreased level?

   - Is she pacing or showing other signs of stress such as clenched fists?

   - Is her face flushed or is she perspiring?

   - Is her breathing increased?

   - Is she repeating herself?

   - Is she yelling or whispering?

   - Are her hands fidgeting more than usual?

   - Is she biting her lips?

   - Is she rubbing her hands along her thighs?

- After she has finished telling you what is on her mind, paraphrase what she has just said (with as little judgment as possible) and ask for confirmation that you heard her correctly.

Listening to your child completely is not only reserved for those times when she has something extremely important to tell you. Listening is *always* important. When your child knows she is being listened to, she feels that what she has to say is important. Your child understands that the thoughts and the feelings that she shares with you are valid, and therefore she is an important and valid person also. Even if she does not have the words or the conscious awareness of this validation, her feelings of self-esteem are deep within and reinforced when you listen.

Listening within the relationship

Listening is important in every relationship. Some children with special needs are non-verbal, so it is important to listen in different ways. In fact, listening to a child's behavior is important, whether she is speaking or not. The numbers vary, but most research on the subject of non-verbal communication agrees that most communication is not done with words; rather, most communication is done with body language and behavior in general (Businesstopia no date).

Teaching empowerment

Teaching our children how to feel strong and empowered is vital for their safety and overall sense of personal strength. To teach our children that they have the same rights as all children, even though they may be smaller than most or not as strong as many, is also a vital lesson. Children with special needs have just as much right to grow up and feel safe as they reach their fullest potential. Although many children with a special need may not achieve generalization of skills, the feeling of being loved and having a sense of confidence and personal power transfers from situation to situation.

Children who are being harmed, either by a family member or another person, begin to feel frightened, weak, powerless, and confused. These feelings impact all aspects of their lives. So, too, feelings of love and empowerment become part of the child and guide her behavior and interactions in all aspects of her life. A child who feels good about herself shows this feeling to the world. She is not as vulnerable as others who don't have the feeling deep inside that she is important.

Assertiveness
Being assertive

Being assertive means that we are aware of a situation and who is involved, and have an expectation of what transpires during a specific interaction. We are active participants in life when we are assertive. We do not allow things to just happen to us. We are not passive.

Not being passive is possible even if your child is dependent for care, as she can participate in the care provided. This participation is observed when a child allows herself to be cared for or provides instruction to the caregiver for her care. This is different from passive behavior, which is when a person gives away all power and allows other people to dictate what is to happen and how any experience will go.

Respect

Having assertiveness skills means moving through the world with respect. Respecting others is important. However, the most important person anyone should be respectful towards is oneself. Respect does not mean to put another person above oneself. Feeling respected is when other people honor who you are and acknowledge that you have the same rights as everyone else.

Being assertive despite a power differential

By acting assertively we understand the role each person has in a given setting and we honor that role. However, at times, actually quite often, a power differential exists. When a child is in school, the teacher is in charge and has a certain amount of power within the classroom. The teacher is responsible for creating the culture of the room. This power is demonstrated by the establishment of a routine and the specific educational experience. The teacher, the other staff, and the students create the environment in the class. It is up to the teacher to communicate what is expected of the students as well as the other staff in the room. If a room is organized and a consistent routine is established, it is easier to know how to behave than if the class is organized in an inconsistent manner.

If a child does not want to listen to the story at the designated time, and acts out with disruptive behaviors, she is not being assertive or respectful; she is being aggressive. The child in this scenario is being disrespectful to the teacher, her fellow classmates and most of all, to herself. She is not honoring the fact that she is in school and the teacher is providing her with the precious gift of education. It is not in her best interests to resist the education she is being offered. We previously acknowledged that all behavior is a form of communication. Teachers in this scenario need to do their best to understand and respond to the specific message that is being sent during a disruptive episode. A calm and assertive response will help the child to recognize that her needs will be met at an appropriate time and in an appropriate way. She does not have the right to disrespect the teacher or her classmates by distracting or delaying the educational process.

When a child who is being disruptive understands that she is being heard, the negative behavior will most likely decrease. Teaching children appropriate and helpful and assertive ways to get their needs met helps them to internalize a sense of personal power and to achieve their individual goals.

Privacy and learning to say "No!"

Privacy was discussed in Chapter 2. Reinforcement of this concept is the core of this issue. While your child now understands the concept of privacy, she must understand how privacy relates to her body. It is also important that she understands that she has the power to control her privacy. She has the right to protect her privacy by saying "No!" if someone wants to invade or assault her privacy. Your child is in charge of who touches her and how it is done (King and King 2010).

Avoiding physical contact

There are many reasons why a child with special needs may not want to be hugged. She may refuse to sit on the lap of a family member. The motive of the family member may be perfectly innocent. If the child is not comfortable and is allowed to have her wishes respected, she will respect herself. She will learn and understand that she has the right to control what happens to her body in regards to others.

If the child is forced to withstand the strong hug (for example) from a relative, she is getting the message that adults have control over how she is treated. She is being taught that her wishes, even her physical discomfort, is secondary to the wishes of the adults around her.

As an occupational therapist I have spent many hours discerning between sensory and behavioral responses. In this instance it is not important to differentiate the reason your child is resistant to the physical offerings, albeit innocent, of a relative; rather it is important that she is listened to and honored. Whether it is because of a sensory sensitivity or another cause, all behavior has a message to communicate. This is especially important in non- or minimally verbal children. So listen to your child by observing and honoring her preferences for touch of all kinds.

The importance of being able to say "No!"

Privacy and being in control of one's body not only refer to private parts or genitals; it is important that your child develops the understanding that she is allowed to have a say in how she is treated physically. Of course it is important that she allows her grandmother, for example, to show her physical affection. It is equally important that that affection be received on your child's terms. Think of it this way: if your child was allergic to bananas, and Grandma's specialty was banana bread, you would not force your child to eat the banana bread to spare Grandma's feelings. Think of an expression of affection in the same way as you would think of the banana bread. Children with an ASD and other special needs are often sensory sensitive. They may not like the physical contact of a hug or the fragrance of the soap another person may use. They may be disturbed by a busy fabric pattern or the sound of many bracelets clanking on a wrist.

If a child is allowed to say "No!" when she is uncomfortable in a situation that is being monitored by you, she is more likely to assert herself when you are not present. Being able to express resistance to being coerced is a valuable tool that children with special needs should have. While many children use "No!" when being offered a non-preferred activity such as teeth brushing or school work, saying "No!", is not all wrong.

It is important to respect the "No!" answer from your child. When a child understands that when you say "No!", as well as when she says "No!", the activity or experience will not happen. Giving your child the understanding that "No!" has great power and should be used only when necessary is a powerful tool. Unfortunately, however, predatory molesters/ abusers are skilled at not taking "No!" for an answer.

Activities for children with an ASD

This is a good activity to do during a calm playtime. The purpose of teaching your child to say "No!" is an important lesson in self-empowerment. Even during play your child will express likes and dislikes. She will make her preferences known, even without words. These expressions may be a physical gesture such as pushing an annoyance away, or a sound, or even the words "Stop!" or "No!"

- During playtime have a plush or otherwise soft toy close by.

- Have the toy tickle or annoy your child, without harming her, of course. You may already know the ways your child enjoys playing and what will annoy her.

- Keep this annoyance slight; you don't want to trigger a tantrum.

- When your child expresses her negative opinion of the interaction, stop the action of the toy. For example, have the toy monkey jump on your child's arm, then stop having the monkey behave in the annoying way when your child expresses her dislike.

- Move the monkey away and ask your child either verbally, or with an icon, or on her communication device if she wants the monkey to tickle her again, or if she enjoys this sort of interaction with the monkey.

- If she does not understand the question, answer for her. Simply say, "You told me 'No!' You do not like the monkey jumping on your arm. The monkey will not jump on your arm again." You can repeat this and reinforce this multiple times over multiple interactions with emphasis on your child's preference of how to play with the toys she enjoys.

It is important that you acknowledge your child's preference and thank her for letting you know. Reinforce for your child that when she tells you "No!" you will listen and if at all possible, comply with her wishes.

Parents know better

During times when your child tells you that she does not want to do something, but you know that for health and safety reasons you simply cannot honor her request and you need to assert your parental rights and responsibilities, it is still important to let her know that you are going to do something (washing her hair, for example) even though she may be saying "No!" Acknowledge that you hear her saying "No!" and explain to her at whatever level she will understand the reason for having her participate in something she does not enjoy.

It is a good idea to understand the reason your child does not want to participate in a self-care activity. Being aware of the sensory issues surrounding most self-care tasks and modifying them to be more palatable to your child will go far in having her comply with her care. Always acknowledge that you hear and understand that your child is adverse to what is taking place. No matter the circumstance, it is important that she knows she is being heard and listened to, if not obeyed.

Activities for children with fluent verbal skills

For the child with fluent verbal skills the word "No!" is most likely in her vocabulary. Your child should learn that this is a powerful word and not to be over-used. Here are some examples you can use to help reinforce the appropriate times and circumstances to use "No!"

- Should I touch a hot pot?

- Should I cut an apple with a sharp knife?

- Should I leave the house to visit a friend without telling my mom?

- Should I let someone in school touch my vagina (penis)?

For some of these, such as household hazards, encourage your child to participate in imaginary play. Your child can play the part of the adult and *teach* a doll the appropriate times and places to use the word "No!"

Discuss this issue as often and as completely as your child wishes.

You can also participate in play to teach your child the times when saying "No!" is not appropriate, such as:

- When Mom asks you to do a chore.

- When it is time to do your homework.

- When it is time for bed.

- When you need to wash your hands, especially after using the bathroom.

There are many times when it is not appropriate for a child to use "No!" as an answer.

As mentioned earlier, if your child balks at the idea of being with someone or attending school or another venue, pay attention. If your child suddenly says "No!" to something, someone, or someplace that in the past she had a neutral response to, attempt to discover the reason for this change.

As your child learns the power of "No!" she is learning to use it appropriately. Honor your child's knowledge of her listening to the voice inside that is doing its best to keep her safe.

Activities for children with a physical disability with typical intelligence

The child with a physical disability learns to maintain her privacy and dignity especially when she requires others to attend to her most personal needs. Having children participate in personal care and therapy when they are as young as possible will help to ensure their safety. The child who knows the routines of her care will be able to appropriately say "No!" when things are not correct.

Activities for children with cognitive impairment and physically typical

Children with cognitive impairment observe the world around them and do their best to emulate what they see. The best way to teach children with a cognitive disability to maintain their privacy is to model the behavior at home. The use of words as well as actions in a multisensory way will help children to integrate the information. With repetition and immediate reinforcement, when behaviors are observed to have been done correctly, this helps to ensure that children have learned the lesson.

Consistent modeling of appropriate behavior

While some families have no problem walking around at home in various stages of undress, this is not a good idea for children with a cognitive impairment. These children will not be able to discern that a specific way to dress, or not, is acceptable in one setting or at one time and situation and not another. For example, if it is okay for dad to come out of the shower and to go into the kitchen wearing only his boxer shorts for coffee on a Sunday morning when only the immediate family is at home, why is it not acceptable for him to walk around in his boxer shorts when guests are in the home?

This is a familiar scenario in many homes, and children who do not have a cognitive disability will understand the nuance presented here. A child with a cognitive disability will not understand the myriad situations that exist. If your child is accustomed to seeing her father, or anyone in the family, walking around in a state of undress, how is she to know that it is wrong when she is in another home and someone is walking around without clothing on?

Predators take their time and get the child accustomed to interactions that cross personal boundaries, such as exhibitionism. They may get pleasure by having a child observe them undressed or touching themselves—even masturbating or exhibiting other sexual behaviors. Giving your child the knowledge to know in no uncertain terms that seeing someone in underwear is not acceptable helps her to say "No!" and maintain her own privacy.

Among the many other accommodations the family with a child with a cognitive impairment must make, teaching privacy by modeling appropriate behaviors and maintaining their own privacy is one that can help your child to increase her own safe conduct. This may be inconvenient and a change in lifestyle, but a change that can be important in the life of your child.

Maintaining privacy and increasing personal power

Teaching your child to maintain her privacy should be a daily occurrence. With repetition your child will learn the importance of her own personal boundaries. When your child is bathing, dressing, or using the toilet, have her do so with the door closed. If you need to help her, you can be in the room with her with the door closed. Make it a point to show her that the door is closed. Even if you are in the room, as she increases her independence, overtly turn away as she wipes her bottom, for example, and tell her that you are turning away so she can have her privacy.

As your child develops skill in personal self-care tasks, continue to reinforce the behaviors that demonstrate the maintenance of her privacy. When she comes out of the toilet, after she has used the room with the door closed, say something like, "Great! I see you protected your privacy by keeping the door shut when you went pee."

Choices

If you think about it, you have the opportunity to present your child with a choice in just about everything she does. Not all choices are monumental—shall I become an occupational therapist or a hair stylist? Most choices are not very important and have no real significance—shall I have coffee or tea? When your child expresses a choice, she has a sense of some control over her experiences.

Choices within required tasks

Some things in life are simply not a choice, especially for children. However, within those instances there are definitely choices. The creative parent needs to find the choice and allow the child to experience the power and rise in self-esteem making that choice provides. For example, your child does not have the choice about going to school. However, she does have the choice of wearing the red sweater or the blue sweater. This way, she is participating in a choice while at the same time following the expectation that she attend school. Perhaps your child is a picky eater. There are certain foods that she simply must eat. Although she does not have the choice about eating these foods, perhaps she has the choice of when during the meal she will eat the food, how the food is prepared, or the sequence in which she will eat. Or perhaps she has the choice of using a spoon or a fork.

Options facilitate personal power

Be mindful of the power of having the chance to make a choice a daily experience. Look for opportunities throughout the day to provide your child with choices. This will give her a sense of power and responsibility. There are times when there is simply not enough time to allow your child to make a decision. Give your child this opportunity as much as possible when it is realistic in the flow of the day. Perhaps in the evening, when the household is calm, you can give your child the choice of the book you will read to her or if she prefers to be read to before or after bath time. You have already decided to participate in these activities with your child, and now that she has some choice in the experience, she has a sense of her own power over her experiences.

As I work with special needs children in the school setting I give my students choices, especially during tasks they don't enjoy. When we are working on writing skills, they do not have the choice to participate in this activity, but they do have the choice of which pencil to use. Once they pick up the pencil, they have made the choice to participate in an activity, although it is not a preference. They know they have chosen a pencil, therefore they are now going to use it to engage in the writing task set before them.

Options and changes may be uncomfortable

Children identified as having an ASD present an interesting challenge when we address the concept of choices. Depending on the intensity of the child's preferences, choices are not something that parents need to think about on a daily basis. Usually the opposite is true. Teaching a child with an ASD that having a choice is not necessarily a bad thing, rather that the opposite can be true, is a challenge.

A choice can be a good thing. In fact, presenting choices and having your child choose between two acceptable options can break her out of the often rigid routines she may be establishing. Helping the child with an ASD and giving her the ability to make a choice can prepare her to be a bit more flexible when situations arise that prevent her routine from being followed precisely, and may even prevent a breakdown. If your child with an ASD gains some skill at making choices, she may be able to handle a choice when it is not her preference to do so.

Here are some activities to help your child gain the skill of making a choice.

Activities for children who are non-verbal or minimally verbal

- At snack time, offer two preferred treats, then:
  - Show your child the containers or actual items.
  - Place both items in front of your child.

- State the one word, "Choose."

- Wait.

- Allow your child to indicate her choice, either by pointing, using a picture icon, or by means of a device (or any means of communication she uses) or reaching for her choice.

- Provide her choice with a big smile.

• At dressing time offer the choice between two different tops, then:

- Hold the tops within her view and reach.

- State the one word, "Choose."

- Wait.

- Allow her to point or touch the one she wants to wear.

- Have her put on the top or assist her in doing so.

- Tell her how great she looks in her choice of top and agree with her decision.

• At story time present two books that she does not usually choose, perhaps new books from the school book fair or the library, then:

- Show her the covers of both books.

- State the one word, "Choose."

- Wait.

- Allow your child to indicate her choice, either by pointing, using a picture icon, or by means of a device (or any means of communication she uses).

- Tell her she has made a good choice.

- Enjoy the book together.

Activities for children with fluent verbal skills

Children with an ASD may have verbal skills beyond their comprehension level. Making choices and going out of a set routine can be stressful for them. The mere fact of choice can at times feel overwhelming. Gently guiding a child with an ASD to make choices will facilitate increased flexibility skills. Once the child is successful and enjoying her choice, she will gain an increased sense of her own power, and her self-esteem will increase as well.

Many children with an ASD process information more easily when the information is presented visually rather than verbally. When practicing making choices in everyday life, it is a good idea to use more visual information than verbal. Use the same techniques as for the non-verbal child, as shown above.

If, in fact, your child initiates a conversation about the choices presented, by all means let her have the lead and discuss the pros and cons of the choices or any other relevant details about her choice. For example, in the snack scenario, perhaps the choice is between ten bite-size cookies or one large cookie.

By all means, if your child is able to discuss the merits of each of her choices, do so. Make an effort to keep her on topic. Point out details of each of the choices she has before her. Discuss the colors or designs of each of the tops she may choose to wear. If the choice is related to books, talk about the nature of the stories or the characters. Depending on the level of sophistication of your child's comprehension, choose as few details as possible with each choice so as not to overwhelm her.

Activities for children with a physical disability with typical intelligence

Children with physical disabilities not only have the motor challenges to overcome, but also a certain amount of misconception about their intellectual abilities. If your child has average intellectual ability, it is important for her to be involved in all the options appropriate to her age and developmental level. Provide her with as many choices as possible during the day.

Pay close attention to life skill areas that may have been overlooked:

- Hygiene care:

  - Fragrance of wipes

  - Sequence of care (that is, teeth cleaning first then toileting, etc.)

- Hair style

- Clothing style

- Splint or brace colors

- Food choices.

Pay very close attention to your child if she is expressing a preference for a particular caregiver or is very resistant to another person. If your child is able to articulate the reasons for her preference, this can help you understand her experiences. When you honor the choices your child makes, she is able to feel her power and control as much as possible in matters that impact her life and daily interactions.

Activities for children who are cognitively impaired and physically typical

Children with cognitive delays who are capable of performing most daily life skills such as bathing, dressing, and feeding themselves may not be able to make the healthiest or most appropriate decisions.

Establish parameters within which your child is able to make what you consider an appropriate choice. For example, your child may want to wear a knitted scarf every day. Although the weather outside is too warm to warrant the wearing of a scarf, this is her choice. She is expressing her sense of style. Ask yourself if there is any harm in the wearing of the scarf. If there is really no problem, then your child's choice of wearing the scarf can give her a sense of her own power. She enjoys the scarf for a multitude of reasons and is being allowed to express her preference. This illustrates a basically harmless way that children can make a choice.

When intentionally thinking about developing your child's choice-making skills, keep the choices simple and at her level of comprehension. For example:

- Offer two choices of a healthy protein for a meal.

- Weather permitting, offer the choice between long or short pants.

- Offer a choice of books for reading time before bed.

- Allow her to choose the sequence of bed time routine (that is, bath first or reading first).

The possibilities are endless throughout the day. Teach your child the words she needs to express her choices. This is an empowering feeling. It may also help with increasing cooperative behavior. If the child has made the choice of which pencil she will use to complete her work, she will have less reason to refuse to do her assignment as she is already engaged in the process.

Activities for children with a physical disability (multiple disabilities)

In this group of children, much of their day is spent at the behest of others. They are fed, clothed, and interacted with on a schedule that is primarily convenient for their caregivers. It is important for all children to know that they have some say in how they are experiencing the world. Here are some areas where choices may be made, even if you are not certain that your child comprehends the process of making a choice:

- Movement: During range of motion (ROM) exercises ask your child if she prefers to move her right arm or left first. Wait for a reply or any sign she has made a choice. Then acknowledge the sign and state, "Alright, you have chosen your right arm to exercise first." The tone of your voice will communicate that you are respecting the child.

- Food choices.

- Bathing/dressing sequences.

Self-esteem and developing competence

The ideas we have about ourselves become a self-fulfilling prophecy. If we believe we can accomplish something— anything at all—we are more likely to accomplish that goal than if we do not believe we are able to at all. This is especially true for children with special needs.

Expectations

High expectations related to the ability level of a child will lead to higher accomplishments. Non-verbal communication reinforces a child's belief about herself and her ability level. When you allow a child to perform a task, you communicate a sense of the belief that the child is capable of completing the task. This helps to increase her confidence in her own skill. For example, if your child is making her bed, and the blanket may not be as straight and tidy as you would have preferred, ask yourself this question: which result is more important, that your child gains the skill and independence in caring for her belongings, or if the bed is neat and tidy?

When a child is continually corrected or not allowed to perform and practice tasks, she will develop a sense of incompetence. This learned helplessness leads to low self-esteem. She begins to have the belief that everyone is smarter and more competent than she is. She then easily yields her power and seeks approval, at times, from inappropriate sources. This makes her more vulnerable to perpetrators who seek children with a weak sense of self. These children are easier to manipulate than those who have confidence and a strong sense of their own power.

Communication to enhance personal power

Using non-verbal communication to let your child know how you feel about her is important. It is also important that you read and correctly interpret her non-verbal communication to understand how she feels. She will communicate a great deal without words. Here are some ways to enhance communication and increase self-esteem in a child with special needs:

- After she has completed any chore around the house, observe if she is smiling and anxious to show you the work. Agree that she did, indeed, complete the job.

- If your child has put any effort into combing her hair, and proudly displays her hairstyle, agree that she does, indeed, look wonderful.

- Look for opportunities to celebrate tasks and the efforts that your child has put into completing them, for example:

  - Setting the table

  - Arts and crafts

  - Dressing

  - Hair brushing

  - School work

  - Sharing with friends

  - Helping to prepare food for the family

  - Being patient when you are not able to respond to a request quickly

  - Toilet training efforts

  - Hand washing.

Remember that there is a fine line between giving children a false sense of their achievement and expecting perfection. You can celebrate the effort while at the same time gently correcting your child's technique.

Use special interests to enhance a strong sense of self

Many children with an ASD develop a special interest; indeed, most children, no matter their cognitive or physical skills, have preferences for certain toys, music, activities, and interactions. These interests are as diverse as the children themselves. Your child may have a special interest in hoses, for example, or she may enjoy playing with a piece of cloth and wrapping it around her body in different ways. Enjoying a special interest with your child is a wonderful way to empower her.

Sharing an interest and allowing the other to lead the play is not unique to children with special needs. Sharing an interest and having the other "teach" you about the interest makes the child feel as though she has something to offer.

A child with good self-esteem is less likely to be coerced or participate in activities that are dangerous to herself or to others. Of course good self-esteem will not prevent all bad things, but it may just be the spark that allows her to fight or tell an adult about an experience that has happened.

Participating in a special interest is one way to help your child have good self-esteem. Showing her love, and expressing genuine happiness when she arrives home from school or even just comes into the room, communicates to her that she is special.

Here are some activities that you may want to try to help boost the self-esteem of your child.

Activities for children who are non-verbal or minimally verbal

Begin by observing your child. Perhaps she is building a block tower with different-colored blocks. As she builds, she strokes each block in a particular way. She continues to play this way for two to three minutes. Now is the time for you to join in. Pick up each block and handle it in the same manner. This is not the time to expand her knowledge about other things she can do with the blocks; remember, she is leading the play. Use minimal language. If your child is non-verbal but is making a sound, repeat that sound. Repeating the sounds a child with an ASD who is non-verbal produces communicates to her that you have heard her and that you are paying attention.

Activities for children with fluent verbal skills

Having you participate in an activity that your child enjoys communicates that she is important. When a busy parent takes the time and pays attention and then allows a child to lead play, this lets her know that her ideas and interests are important.

Take care to not act impatiently. Do not look at your watch or phone during this play period. The time you set aside to play with your child in this way can be as little as 10–15 minutes, although you can, of course, also play and interact with your child at other times during the day. This specific interaction is specifically designed for you to boost your child's self-esteem. Be present and fully engaged with your child. Nothing makes a person—any person—feel more important than when someone pays full attention to them.

- With gestures or facial expressions, ask your child for help. Perhaps hand her a block from your pile and show her that you would like her to work on your tower as well. If your child enjoys hugs, hug her as she plays. Tell your child in whatever manner she understands that you are proud of her and what she is able to accomplish. Thank her for the help she has provided in the building of your tower.

- If your child is verbal and enjoys sorting toys, blocks, or crayons by color, for example, this is another wonderful circumstance when you can help build your child's feeling of self-worth. After she has sorted the crayons and perhaps named the colors, join in. Again, this is not the time to challenge your child; rather, in this instance, as you are helping her gain a sense of self-worth, give her some other items that you know she is able to name and sort as well. Provide that success experience for her.

- If you believe she is ready, you may challenge her by teaching her other color names, for example, pink or light blue. As she names and sorts these colored items, provide positive comments about how smart she is.

Experiences to provide success

Allowing your child to experience success after being challenged by something that causes her to stretch her skills just a bit is extremely powerful. Remember, this is not the time when you are teaching your child a new skill; rather, it is a time when she uses the skills she has already mastered and is able to demonstrate her skill.

Here are a few ideas that your child with an ASD may be able to participate in to show you her competency. While participating in these activities, she can build her self-esteem. Remember to encourage her to do something she enjoys and is able to do (she does not need to be perfect or even have a high level of competency; she just needs to feel good when she is participating in the activity):

- Sorting shapes, colors, laundry (types of clothing)— the variety is endless

- Lining up cars or trucks

- Building, with LEGO®, blocks, etc.

- Scissor skills (cutting out various pictures from magazines, for example)

- Helping with chores around the house

- Tidying her room

- Reading

- Coloring

- Self-care skills

- Exercises (bicycle riding, yoga, climbing, swinging)

- Anything she enjoys…

Break down activities into small, achievable parts that you know your child is able to accomplish without any help.

Activities for children with a physical disability and typical intelligence

Children with average or above-average intelligence who need assistance with mobility or methods to decrease tremors are often in general education settings. They may excel at specific academic subjects while not being able to compete or even participate in various sports or recreational activities with their peers. It is not enough to tell them that they are smart and the other things don't matter. Self-esteem is felt deep within the individual.

- Modifying activities or equipment for children with a physical disability is an important way to encourage engagement. Participation in group sports or craft activities helps all children to develop a healthy sense of self.

- Many sports activities are done in a wheelchair; rugby and basketball are two very competitive sports that can be played seated. Many types of cycles can be adapted to allow children with limited physical skill to feel the independence of moving freely. Look up videos of the Paralympics for inspiration.

- If your child is using a wheelchair, it is important that she be able to propel the chair independently. When a child is able to move throughout a school campus, just as her peers do, she is able to gain a feeling of competency and independence. She is able to choose where she goes and is in control of getting there.

All children should be encouraged to pursue their strengths and interests. Perhaps they have an interest in science or chess. Adapting methods of tool use or movement of chess pieces may at times require creativity, but can certainly be accomplished. You only need to learn about the great scientist Stephen Hawking for inspiration.

Activities for children with a cognitive impairment and physically typical

Children with excellent motor skills may not have the competency to complete tasks that are more than one or two steps. Despite current efforts at inclusive education and the integration of children of all ability levels into mainstream groups, children with a cognitive impairment are aware of the differences between themselves and other children. These become obvious in a variety of ways, such as:

- Your child may need additional time to complete a project.

- A school project may be obviously simplified.

- Your child may need the steps of a project broken down into manageable chunks.

- She may not be able to properly sequence activities.

- Your child may need assistance to use tools safely.

- Your child may have difficulty expressing herself verbally.

- Your child may have a difficult time coming up with her own ideas for a written assignment or a craft project; she may copy others.

Adapting projects to assure success can be done in the following ways:

- Provide guidelines for your child to work within, such as outlining a picture to be colored in or using a sentence starter for a writing assignment.

- If your child is working on a craft such as a beading or needlework project, use larger or firmer materials that do not require fine motor dexterity.

- Set simple short-term goals with your child and help her to see and celebrate her success along the way with the completion of each step. For example, if she is helping to prepare a meal:

  - Have her place the salad ingredients on the counter.

  - Have her tear the lettuce and place it in the bowl.

- Have her add the other veggies that you have chopped (or she has prepared, as appropriate).

- Have her add the dressing.

- Enjoy a job well done!

Any undertaking can be broken down into its component parts.

Encouraging independence enhances self-esteem

Focus on the tasks that you know your child is able to do independently. Whenever feasible, leave your child alone to complete these tasks. Allow her to present you with her completed project. Take the cues of her non-verbal communication when she is showing that she has a sense of pride. Even if, for example, the salad she has prepared is not exactly to your liking, or the words are not written exactly on the line, if your child believes she has done a good job, agree.

Congratulate her on the obvious effort she put into her work. Let her know that you are able to see the excellent care and time she took to achieve her goal. There is time enough later for her to practice her skill and to increase her functional level.

By encouraging her, and not always pointing out places for improvement, she will feel good about her efforts. When your child feels good about her efforts, her sense of confidence will grow. With confidence she increases her belief that the next time she attempts anything, she will be successful. Even if she is not successful the next time, the fact that she had the experience of feeling good about herself will not be extinguished. She will continue to work hard to experience that wonderful feeling of putting in a good effort again.

Activities for children with multiple disabilities

Depending on the level of disability, a child with multiple disabilities will most likely have a number of caregivers. Some will be with your child for years, while others will be with her for only a short time. No matter the time frame, a few important points are vital to share so that your child can feel good about herself. Non-verbal communication is important in how parents and caregivers interact with your child. Remember and share these essential concepts:

- Don't rush the care: Whether your child is being fed or read to, it is important to interact at a calm pace. Children pick up tension from other people. If your child is being rushed she is less likely to feel calm and may not respond or be cooperative with the task at hand.

- Be mindful of what you are doing when interacting with your child: Put away your smartphone, turn off the television, and simply pay attention to your child and the activity you and your child are engaged in at the time.

- Increase your self-awareness: When you are interacting with your child, notice if you are tense, distracted by something else going on in your life, or anything at all. No one is able to be at their best all the time. Know when you are not feeling up to a challenge, and slow your pace and simplify your interactions if at all possible.

- Take care of yourself: Being a caregiver for a child with multiple disabilities is an all-encompassing life. Make sure you get enough rest, nutrition, and exercise. Ask for help.

- If things are not going right, or you are feeling frustrated, do not take out your anger on your child. It is not her fault.

- Pay attention to your child's responses: If she can verbalize or physically respond in any way, acknowledge this. Give your child positive feedback and let her know that you understand what she is communicating to you. This feedback can provide a great sense of connection and support. Feedback and support makes anyone feel good.

- Talk to your child: Even if you don't think she can comprehend what you are saying, we cannot underestimate the value of the connection with each other.

- Do not ignore your child as you are interacting with her.

- Do not have conversations with other people in front of your child that you would not want to be repeated.

- If caregivers act as though they are being observed, their behavior may become more responsible.

These are great concepts to help raise your child's self-esteem, no matter what her functional level may be. The most able-bodied or cognitively typical child will benefit from these ideas.

Creating experiences of success

In the field of occupational therapy we use the concept of the "just right" challenge to encourage participation and enthusiasm for a specific activity. The idea is that if a task is too easy, the child will become easily bored, lose interest, and move on to something else. If a task is too difficult, she will give up, feel like a failure, become frustrated, and not want to engage in similar activities in the future.

Discovering the "just right" challenge

To discover your child's "just right" challenge, observe how she is completing a specific task. For example, she may be working on a puzzle that has an outline of the form of each piece that the specific puzzle piece is to be located in. Perhaps the puzzle has eight pieces, and this is simple for your child to complete, and she does so quickly. One way to give her a challenge is to ask her if she can complete the puzzle she just finished outside of the existing framework. Another way to increase the challenge level is to offer puzzles with 10 or 12 pieces. The increased level of puzzle completion examples are the "just right" challenge because you know she understands and is able to demonstrate the concept of puzzle completion; you are just increasing the difficulty level.

Small steps lead to big accomplishments

Another method to help your child increase skill while engaged in daily living activities is to break each part of the task into small and manageable steps. If your child is learning to dress herself, don't just expect her to take all the clothing she needs for the day out of her dresser, put them on with all the buttons and zippers done, and have them in the correct orientation and be appropriate for the setting she will be attending (school versus church) and correct for the weather (she has not chosen to wear a snow suit to go to the beach in the summer).

Breaking down each task into manageable parts, and not increasing the expectation of skill competency until she has demonstrated that she is able to complete each prior step, will give her a sense of competency and increase her self-esteem.

Remember that children with special needs require repetition and consistency to learn new skills. Give her the amount of time she needs and be patient. Her self-esteem will grow when she is allowed to complete tasks for herself in her own time frame. Losing patience and saying something such as "It will just be faster if I do it myself!" can be devastating to the child's self-esteem and inhibit her from attempting new tasks in the future.

Of course there will be times when you simply do not have the time needed for the child to practice her independent skill growth. In these instances, explain to your child that on this day you need to help her because you need to get to work early, or whatever explanation you have that does not blame your child for the rushed morning.

Break down dressing tasks this way:

- Look outside to determine the weather.

- Choose clothing with your child that would be appropriate to wear on that day.

- Have her take underwear and socks from the dresser; it is a good idea for clothing to be within reach of your child, as this increases her opportunity for independence.

- Have her take off her night clothing, or if she bathes in the morning, have the clothing you have chosen together near the area where she dries off or in the bathroom.

- Begin by encouraging her to dress in her underwear first; if she is about to put it on backwards, give her a clue about the shape of the garment or placement of the label so she can recognize front and back.

- Continue the above steps with each article of clothing, only correcting her dressing skill if she is attempting to put on a garment inside out or backwards; straightening out an article of clothing to perfection is not as important as allowing your child to feel independent and competent.

If your child has great difficulty with the first article of clothing, work on that only, and then complete dressing her. Continue to allow her to practice dressing daily. With practice she will gain skill. If she is willing, and you have the time, allow her to attempt donning other articles of clothing, helping her to complete the job only when she requests help. If she shows a great interest in putting on a sweater, for example, after she has dressed, allow her to experiment with this skill.

All children learn best when they are interested in the experience. The more practice the child has with moving her body in the specific motions needed to dress, the more competent she will become in the process.

Children learn best when they have people around them who believe that they can accomplish great things. Give your child the opportunity to grow into the best version of herself that she possibly can. When your child has the belief that she is a worthwhile and wonderful member of the planet, she will possibly have the strength to inhibit those who want to harm her.

A List of Alternative Pronunciations

This is a list of alternative pronunciations to be used if your child is unable to pronounce words for genitalia accurately. The main thing is to be consistent.

Anus

- an
- nus
- us

Breast

- b
- est
- bret
- best
- rest

Foreskin

- forekin
- fork

- forkin
- forks
- orkin
- orskin
- skin
- in
- fskin
- f-in

Lips

- ips
- li

Mouth

- mmm
- outh
- mout
- mth

Nipple

- nip
- nips
- ip
- ips

Penis

- p

- peen
- enis
- is
- nis

Rectum

- rec
- tum
- rtum
- um

Testicles

- tests
- test
- est
- ticles
- t-icle
- icles
- icle
- le

Tongue

- to
- tog
- noung
- nog

Urethra

- u
- ur
- thra
- tra
- u-thra
- u-tra

Vagina

- vinga
- ina
- vag
- ag
- gina

Resources Guide

This guide is to serve as information only. The products and other references presented here are for informational purposes only, and do not constitute an endorsement of specific products by Debra S. Jacobs or Jessica Kingsley Publishers.

Advocacy centers
Canada
Child and Youth Advocacy Centres (information is provided in English and French): Cac-cae.ca

United States
National Children's Advocacy Center (1037 centers across the US): www.nationalcac.org

Europe
Eurochild: www.eurochild.org

United Kingdom
National Youth Advocacy Service: www.nyas.net

Global

International Society for the Prevention of Child Abuse and Neglect (ISPCAN): Ispcan.org

Free apps for smartphones

ASSIST: logs student results to any assessment type.

Child Safety, Good Touch & Bad Touch: educating children about good or bad touches.

Kid Call: designed by a parent for parents, this app makes it possible for little ones to make emergency or just-for-fun phone, FaceTime or Skype calls.

WebWatcher: free parental control and phone tracker.

Books

Don't Call Me Special: A First Look at Disability by Pat Thomas, illustrated by Lesley Harker

Stephen Hawking and the Universe: A Biography by Ben Sztajnkrycer

Equipment

Hands-free cath mirror: www.healthproductsforyou.com

Shelters

Canada

Shelter Safe (information available in all the territories and provided in English and French as well as aboriginal languages): www.sheltersafe.ca

United States

The National Domestic Violence Hotline (Spanish information available): www.thehotline.org

United Kingdom

Shelter England: https://england.shelter.org.uk

National Domestic Violence Helpline: 0808-2000-247

Women's Aid (find local help by putting in your location on the resource list): www.womensaid.org

Global

Many cities have shelters available; ask local law enforcement or search the internet for a safe place for you and your children.

References and Further Reading

Baker, J.E. (2003) *Social Skills Training.* Shawnee Mission, KS: Autism Asperger Publishing Company.

Brown, D. (2008) *The Aspie Girl's Guide to Being Safe with Men.* London and Philadelphia, PA: Jessica Kingsley Publishers.

Brown, L.K. and Brown, M. (1998) *How to Be a Friend.* New York: Hachette Book Group.

Businesstopia (no date) 'Why is non-verbal communication important?' Available at www.businesstopia.net/communication/why-non-verbal-communication-important, accessed on July 6, 2018.

Carol Gray Social Stories (2018) 'What Is a Social Story?' Available at https://carolgraysocialstories.com/social-stories/what-is-it, accessed on July 6, 2018.

Coloplast.us (no date) 'How-to Catheter Guides for Children.' Available at www.coloplast.us/bladder-and-bowel/how-to-guides/catheter-guides-for-children/#section=This-how-to-guide-is-for-girls-in-a-wheelchair-using-a-SpeediCath%c2%ae-Compact-catheter._240044, accessed on July 6, 2018.

Darkness to Light (2018) 'End Child Sexual Abuse.' Available at www.d2l.org, accessed on July 6, 2018.

Dorightbykids.org (2003) 'Who is Mandated to Report?' Available at www.dorightbykids.org/am-i-a-mandated-reporter/who-is-mandated-to-report, accessed on July 6, 2018.

Jacobs, D.S. (2015) 'The goals of "girls" group.' *Advance for Occupational Therapy Practitioners,* February 15–16.

Jacobs, D.S. and Betts, D.E. (2012) *Everyday Activities to Help Your Young Child with Autism Live Life to the Full.* London and Philadelphia, PA: Jessica Kingsley Publishers.

King, Z. and King, K. (2010). *I Said No!* Weaverville, CA: Boulden Publishing.

Merriam-Webster (2018) 'Friendly.' Available at www.merriam-webster.com/dictionary/friendly, accessed on July 6, 2018.

National Center for Victims of Crime (2012) 'Child Sexual Abuse Statistics.' Available at http://victimsofcrime.org/media/reporting-on-child-sexual-abuse/child-sexual-abuse-statistics, accessed on July 6, 2018.

Quotes about 'Friendship' available at www.goodreads.com/quotes/tag/friendship, accessed on July 6, 2018.

Sanders, J. (2015) *No Means No!* Macclesfield, VIC, Australia: Upload Publishing.

Sapolsky, R.M. (1994) *Why Zebras Don't Get Ulcers.* New York: Henry Holt & Company.

Scouts.ca (no date) 'The Two Scouter Rule and Section Ratios: Supervision for Scouting Programs.' Available at www.scouts.ca/sites/default/files/Two-Scouter-Rule.pdf, accessed on July 6, 2018.

SlideShare (2015) 'Goodenough Scoring (Psychometrics).' Available at www.slideshare.net/hawraaalromani/goodenough-scoring-psychometrics, accessed on July 6, 2018.

Spelman, C. (1997) *Your Body Belongs to You.* Chicago, IL: Albert Whitman & Company.

Stop It Now! (no date) Tip Sheet: 'Child Sexual Abuse Prevention for Faith Communities.' Available at www.stopitnow.org/ohc-content/tip-sheet-10, accessed on July 6, 2018.

Swanton, J. (2017) 'Sexual health education: Developing and implementing a curriculum for adolescents and young adults with intellectual disabilities.' *OT Practice 22,* 19, 14–17.

The Scout Group (2011) Chapter 3. Available at https://members.scouts.org.uk/media/761074/Chapter-3.pdf, accessed on July 6, 2018.

Tobin, P. and Kessner, S.L. (2002) *Keeping Kids Safe.* Alameda, CA: Hunter House Publishers.

True Tolerance (2018) 'Parents' Bill of Rights for Public Schools.' Available at www.truetolerance.org/2012/parents-bill-of-rights-for-public-schools, accessed on July 6, 2018.

UN (United Nations) (1989) Convention on the Rights of the Child. Adopted and opened for signature, ratification and accession by General Assembly Resolution 44/25 of 20 November.

Voices Carry Child Advocacy Center (no date) 'Medical exam, what to expect.' Available at www.voicescarrycac.org/programs-services/medical-exam-what-to-expect, accessed on July 6, 2018.

Western Psychological Services (2012) *Protocol for the ADOS-2.* Torrance, CA.

White, S.W. (2011) *Social Skills Training for Children with Asperger Syndrome and High-Functioning Autism.* New York and London: The Guilford Press.

Index

Index

CPI Antony Rowe
Eastbourne, UK
October 10, 2022